Walled States, Waning Sovereignty

Walled States,
Waning Sovereignty

Wendy Brown

ZONE BOOKS · NEW YORK

2010

ZONE BOOKS
1226 Prospect Avenue
Brooklyn, NY 11218

Printed in the United States of America.

Distributed by The MIT Press,
Cambridge, Massachusetts, and London, England

Library of Congress Cataloging-in-Publication Data

Brown, Wendy, 1955–
    Walled states, waning sovereignty / Wendy Brown.
        p. cm.
    Includes bibliographical references and index.
    ISBN 978-1-935408-08-6
        1. Sovereignty. 2. Nation-state. 3. Globalization—
Political aspects. 4. Border security. 5. Boundaries. I. Title.

    JC327.B75 2010
    320.1–dc22

                            2009053279

Contents

CHAPTER ONE

Waning Sovereignty,

Walled Democracy

Fortification as the defense of places ended for all practical purposes with the breaching of the Atlantik Wall in 1944. Thereafter, formal fortifications as a principal means of defence, even on the most extensive scale, were obsolete.
—Paul Hirst, *Space and Power*

We need soft borders, not rigid impermeable ones.... At the threshold of the twenty-first century, we do not need to reinforce sovereignty.
—Shimon Peres, *The New Middle East*

I told them: don't build fences around your settlements. If you put up a fence, you put a limit to your expansion. We should place the fences around the Palestinians and not around our places.
—Ariel Sharon, quoted in Neve Gordon, *Israel's Occupation*

It is not the wall that has created the camp, but rather the strategy and reality of encampment which has led to the construction of the wall.
—Adi Ophir and Ariella Azoulay, "The Monster's Tail"

Fortresses are generally much more harmful than useful.
—Niccoló Machiavelli, *The Discourses on The First Ten Books of Titus Livius*

What we have come to call a globalized world harbors fundamental tensions between opening and barricading, fusion and partition, erasure and reinscription. These tensions materialize as increasingly liberalized borders, on the one hand, and the devotion of unprecedented funds, energies, and technologies to border fortification, on the other. Globalization features a host of related tensions between global networks and local nationalisms, virtual power and physical power, private appropriation and open sourcing, secrecy and transparency, territorialization and deterritorialization. It also features tensions between national interests and the global market, hence between the nation and the state, and between the security of the subject and the movements of capital.

One place these tensions nest is in the new walls striating the globe, walls whose frenzied building was underway even as the crumbling of the old bastilles of Cold War Europe and apartheid South Africa was being internationally celebrated. Best known are the United States-built behemoth along its southern border and the Israeli-built wall snaking through the West Bank, two projects that share technology, subcontracting, and also refer to each other for legitimacy.[1] But there are many others. Post-apartheid South Africa features a complex internal maze of walls and checkpoints and maintains a controversial electrified security barrier on its Zimbabwe border. Saudi Arabia recently finished constructing a ten-foot-high concrete post structure along its border with Yemen, which will be followed by a wall at the Iraq border, which in turn Saudis say may be followed by walling their whole country. To deter refugees from its poorer neighbors, to stake its side in a land dispute, and to suppress the movement of Islamic guerillas and weapons across its Pakistan border, cruder barriers have been built by India to wall out Pakistan, Bangladesh, and Burma and to wall in disputed Kashmir territory.[2] The crudeness should not deceive: India has mined the land space between double layers of barbed and concertina wire along the Indo-Kashmir border. Also in the context of a land dispute, but officially built in the name of interdicting "Islamic terrorists," Uzbekistan fenced out Kyrgyzstan in 1999 and Afghanistan in 2001, but Turkmenistan is now fencing out Uzbekistan. Botswana initiated the building of an electric fence along its border with

Barrier around the Spanish enclave of Melilla in Morocco (Chiara Tamburini).

U.S.-Mexico border (David McNew/Getty Images).

U.S.-Mexico border (Marc Silver).

The Israeli Wall in the area of Qalandiya, North Jerusalem (Sebastian Bolesch).

The Israeli wall enclosing Bethlehem (Musa Al-Shaer/AFP/Getty Images).

India-Bangladesh border fence (Veronique de Viguerie/Getty Images).

India-Pakistan border fence (Ami Vitale/Getty Images).

Saudi barrier at the border with Yemen (Khaled Fazaa/AFP/Getty Images).

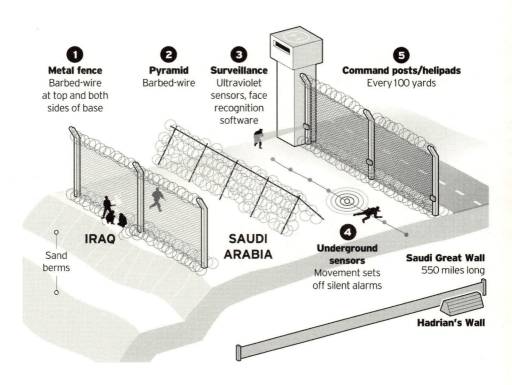

1 Metal fence
Barbed-wire at top and both sides of base

2 Pyramid
Barbed-wire

3 Surveillance
Ultraviolet sensors, face recognition software

5 Command posts/helipads
Every 100 yards

IRAQ

SAUDI ARABIA

Sand berms

4 Underground sensors
Movement sets off silent alarms

Saudi Great Wall
550 miles long

Hadrian's Wall

Diagram of a 550-mile barrier being built by Saudi Arabia on its border with Iraq (Ciaran Hughes).

Barrier separating Shiite and Sunni neighborhoods of al-Shula and al-Ghazaliyeh in Baghdad
(Ali Al-Saadi/AFP/Getty Images).

Zimbabwe in 2003, ostensibly to stop the spread of foot-and-mouth disease among livestock, but aimed at interdicting Zimbabwean humans, as well. In response to the south Thailand insurgency and to deter illegal immigration and smuggling, Thailand and Malaysia have cooperated to build a concrete and steel border wall. The wall between Egypt and Gaza was brought to the world's attention when it was breached in January 2008 by Gazans seeking food, fuel, and other domestic goods. Iran is walling out Pakistan. Brunei is walling out immigrants and smugglers coming from Limbang. China is walling out North Korea to stem the tide of Korean refugees, but parallel to one section of this wall, North Korea is also walling out China.

There are walls within walls: Gated communities in the United States have sprung up everywhere, but are especially plentiful in Southwestern cities near the wall with Mexico. Walls around Israeli settlements in the West Bank abut the "security barrier," and walls around the disputed Museum of Tolerance site in Jerusalem nestle next to walls partitioning that city. Bethlehem has been completely sealed off from Jerusalem with towering concrete walls. The European Union sponsors triple-layer walls around Spanish enclaves in Morocco even as Morocco itself maintains a lengthy "berm" aimed at securing the resources of the long-disputed Western Sahara. And in the name of preventing what he termed "French situations," the socialist mayor of Padua recently built the Via Anelli Wall to separate white middle-class neighborhoods from the so-called "African ghetto" where most new immigrants live.

Still more walls are coming: Notwithstanding the dustup in 2007 over a proposed Baghdad wall, the United States military still hopes to wall the territory marked by the Green Line in that city. It has already built controversial walls around Sunni neighborhoods such as Adhamiya and Azamya, modeling the beginning of Iraqi urban "gated communities" in response to the bloody sectarian violence unleashed by the U.S. occupation.[3] Brazil plans to build a steel-and-concrete wall along its border with Paraguay, Israel plans to replace an old fence with a security barrier across its Sinai Desert border with Egypt, and the United Arab Emirates is designing a wall for its Oman border. Kuwait has a fence, but wants a wall in the demilitarized zone approximating its border with Iraq. Serious proposals have been floated to follow completion of the U.S.-Mexico wall with one along the Canadian border and also to find a means of barricading the islands that provide conduits to Europe from would-be North African migrants.

If these walls vary in what they aim to deter—poor people, workers, or asylum seekers; drugs, weapons, or other contraband; smuggled taxable goods; kidnapped or enslaved youth; terror; ethnic or religious mixing; peace and other political futures—there are surely common dimensions to their proliferation at this moment in world history. Let us start with a series of paradoxes. First, even as those across a wide political spectrum— neoliberals, cosmopolitans, humanitarians, and left activists— fantasize a world without borders (whether consequent to global entrepreneurship, global markets, global citizenship, or global governance), nation-states, rich and poor, exhibit a passion for wall building. Second, within the ostensibly triumphant universal political form, democracy (heralded by European post-Marxists, Islamic secularists, or American neoconservatives, even if each inflects democracy differently), we confront not only barricades, but passageways through them segregating high-end business traffic, ordinary travelers, and aspiring entrants deemed suspect by virtue of origin or appearance.[4] Third, in a time featuring capacities for destruction historically unparalleled in their combined potency, miniaturization, and mobility, from bodies wired for explosion to nearly invisible biochemical toxins, these deadly but incorporeal powers are perversely answered by the stark physicalism of walls. So, three paradoxes: one featuring simultaneous opening and blocking, one featuring universalization combined with exclusion and stratification, and one featuring networked and virtual power met by physical barricades.

What is also striking about these new barriers is that even as they limn or attempt to define nation-state boundaries, they are not built as defenses against potential attacks by other sovereigns, as fortresses against invading armies, or even as shields against weapons launched in interstate wars. Rather, while the particular danger may vary, these walls target nonstate transnational actors—individuals, groups, movements, organizations, and industries. They react to transnational, rather than international relations and respond to persistent, but often informal or subterranean powers, rather than to military undertakings. The migration, smuggling, crime, terror, and even political purposes that walls would interdict are rarely state sponsored, nor, for the most part, are they incited by national interests. Rather, they take shape apart from conventions of Westphalian international order in which sovereign nation-states are the dominant political actors. As such, they appear as signs of a post-Westphalian world.

To speak of a post-Westphalian order is not to imply an era in which nation-state sovereignty is either finished or irrelevant. Rather, the prefix "post" signifies a formation that is *temporally after but not over* that to which it is affixed. "Post" indicates a very particular condition of afterness in which what is past is not left behind, but, on the contrary, relentlessly conditions, even dominates a present that nevertheless also breaks in some way with this past. In other words, we use the term "post" only for a present whose past continues to capture and structure it. Thus did "post-War" characterize much of the second half of the Euro-Atlantic twentieth century, just as "post-Communism" identifies political, social, and economic challenges and predicaments set by the former Soviet bloc, while "post-Marxism" gathers contemporary diverse strands of left philosophy and analysis working in the long shadow of Marxist intellectual paradigms and political attachments.

Given the vigorousness with which states still assert sovereign power and their importance in constituting global order and disorder, what is meant by the claim that state sovereignty is waning?[5] This will be explored in Chapter 2. Here, we may simply note that a composite figure of sovereignty drawn from classical theorists of modern sovereignty, including Thomas Hobbes, Jean Bodin, and Carl Schmitt, suggests that sovereignty's indispensable features include supremacy (no higher power), perpetuity over time (no term limits), decisionism (no boundedness by or submission to law), absoluteness and completeness (sovereignty cannot be probable or partial), nontransferability (sovereignty cannot be conferred without canceling itself), and specified jurisdiction (territoriality).[6] If nation-state sovereignty has always been something of a fiction in its aspiration and claim to these qualities, the fiction is a potent one and has suffused the internal and external relations of nation-states since its consecration by the 1648 Peace of Westphalia. However, over the past half century, the monopoly of these combined attributes by nation-states has been severely compromised by growing transnational flows of capital, people, ideas, goods, violence, and political and religious fealty. These flows both tear at the borders they cross and crystallize as powers within them, thus compromising sovereignty from its edges and from its interior. Nation-state sovereignty has been undercut as well by neoliberal rationality, which recognizes no sovereign apart from entrepreneurial decision makers (large and small), which displaces legal and political principles (especially liberal commitments to universal inclusion, equality, liberty, and the rule of law) with market criteria, and which demotes the political sovereign to managerial status. Nation-state sovereignty has also been eroded by the steady growth and importance of international economic and governance institutions such as the International Monetary Fund and World Trade Organization. And nation-state sovereignty has been challenged by a quarter century of postnational and international assertions of law, rights, and authority that sometimes openly aim to subvert or supersede the sovereignty of states.[7]

While it is no news that nation-state sovereignty is challenged by global movements of capital and the growing power of transnational legal, economic, and political institutions, the other forces mentioned above are less often recognized as part of political sovereignty's contemporary undoing. These include the political rationalities of neoliberalism, transnational moral and legal discourses, along with activations of power related to, but not reducible to capital—those that traffic under the sign of culture, ideology, and religion. Meanwhile, forces sustaining or shoring up nation-state sovereignty are few and tend to be backward looking—for example, nationalism, despotism, and imperialism.

The effect of these combined developments is not to eliminate sovereignty from the political map or to enter either a postsovereign or poststate era. As nation-state sovereignty wanes, states and sovereignty do not simply decline in power or significance, but instead come apart from one another. States persist as nonsovereign actors, and many characteristics of sovereignty (though not its intact theological form) appear today in two domains of power that are, not coincidentally, the very transnational domains of powers that the Peace of Westphalia emerged to contain within or subordinate to nation-states: political economy and religiously legitimated violence. Thus, in contrast with Michael Hardt's and Antonio Negri's claim that nation-state sovereignty has transformed into global Empire, and in contrast with Giorgio Agamben's thesis that sovereignty has metamorphosed into the worldwide production and sacrifice of bare life (global civil war), I argue that key characteristics of sovereignty are migrating from the nation-state to the unrelieved domination of capital and God-sanctioned political violence. Neither capital nor God-sanctioned violence bows to another power; both are indifferent to and/or tacticalize domestic as well as international law; both spurn or supervene juridical norms; both recuperate the promise of sovereignty: *E pluribus unum*. As for decisionism, the signature characteristic of sovereignty identified by Carl Schmitt, both capital and theological governance have the capacity to be decisive without being decisionist, suggesting that it may be only in sovereignty's specifically political instantiation in states that a "decider" (as George W. Bush referred to himself, perhaps intimating the

23

parodic element of a form in its death throes) is essential. Certainly if Schmitt is right that political sovereignty derives from a theological version, it is significant that God's sovereignty is not decisionist—it simply *is*.

In sum, in a post-Westphalian order, sovereign nation-states no longer exclusively define the field of global political relations or monopolize many of the powers organizing that field, yet states remain significant actors in that field, as well as symbols of national identification. This book argues that the new nation-state walls are iconographic of this predicament of state power. Counterintuitively, perhaps, it is the weakening of state sovereignty, and more precisely, the detachment of sovereignty from the nation-state, that is generating much of the frenzy of nation-state wall building today. Rather than resurgent expressions of nation-state sovereignty, the new walls are icons of its erosion. While they may appear as hyperbolic tokens of such sovereignty, like all hyperbole, they reveal a tremulousness, vulnerability, dubiousness, or instability at the core of what they aim to express—qualities that are themselves antithetical to sovereignty and thus elements of its undoing.[8] Hence the visual paradox of these walls: What appears at first blush as the articulation of state sovereignty actually expresses its diminution relative to other kinds of global forces—the waning relevance and cohesiveness of the form.

Rather than iterations of nation-state sovereignty, the new nation-state walls are part of an ad hoc global landscape of flows and barriers both inside nation-states and in the surrounding postnational constellations, flows and barriers that divide richer from poorer parts of the globe. This landscape signifies the ungovernability by law and politics of many powers unleashed by globalization and late modern colonialization, and a resort to policing and blockading in the face of this ungovernability. These are powers that possess discernible logics, but that lack political form or organization, let alone subjective and coordinated intentionality.[9] Indeed, insofar as the new walls at the edges of

nation-states articulate with other barriers and forms of surveillance, private and public, they signal the existence of a corrupted
divide between internal and external policing and between the
police and the military. This, in turn, suggests an increasingly
blurred distinction between the inside and outside of the nation
itself, and not only between criminals within and enemies without. (Such blurring is emblematized by the growing movement
in the United States to criminalize and imprison, rather than
deport undocumented migrants.) Thus, one irony of late modern
walling is that a structure taken to mark and enforce an inside/
outside distinction—a boundary between "us" and "them" and
between friend and enemy—appears as precisely the opposite
when grasped as part of a complex of eroding lines between the
police and the military, subject and *patria*, vigilante and state, law
and lawlessness.

Seen from a slightly different angle, as responses to contested
and eroding state sovereignty, the new walls project an image of
sovereign jurisdictional power and an aura of the bounded and
secure nation that are at the same time undercut by their existence and also by their functional inefficacy. Notwithstanding
their strikingly physicalist and obdurate dimensions, the new
walls often function theatrically, projecting power and effica-
ciousness that they do not and cannot actually exercise and that
they also performatively contradict. To literalize walls as pure
interdiction occludes their production of an imago of sovereign
state power in the face of its undoing, and it occludes the walls'
consecration of the corruption, contestation, or violation of the
borders they would fortify. It also misses their staging of sovereign powers of protection, powers radically limited by modern
technologies and paths of infiltration and by the dependence of
various "national economies" on much of what walls purport to
lock out, especially cheap labor. It misses, in short, the Wizard
of Oz quality in the new walls, the way they echo coded (yellow/
orange/red) security threat levels that stage an image of state
intelligence and control in the face of the opposite.

This theatricalized and spectacularized performance of sovereign power at aspirational or actual national borders brings into relief nation-state sovereignty's theological remainder. If walls do not actually accomplish the interdiction fueling and legitimating them, if they perversely institutionalize the contested and degraded status of the boundaries they limn, they nevertheless stage both sovereign jurisdiction and an aura of sovereign power and awe. Walls thus bear the irony of being mute, material, and prosaic, yet potentially generative of theological awe largely unrelated to their quotidian functions or failures.

The striking popular desire for walling today, considered in light of recent pejorative historical associations with walling and with contemporary walling's general inefficacy vis-à-vis its putative aims, can be traced to an identification with and anxiety about this sovereign impotence. The popular desire for walling harbors a wish for the powers of protection, containment, and integration promised by sovereignty, a wish that recalls the theological dimensions of political sovereignty. If the fiction of state sovereignty is the secularization of the fiction of divine power, the deteriorating viability of this political fiction generates understandable popular anxiety, an anxiety addressed in part by the theological effect and affect of walling. The detachment of sovereign powers from nation-states also threatens an imaginary of individual and national identity dependent upon perceivable horizons and the containment they offer. Thus, walls generate what Heidegger termed a "reassuring world picture" in a time increasingly lacking the horizons, containment, and security that humans have historically required for social and psychic integration and for political membership.

In the remainder of this chapter, I argue for the validity of conceiving the new walls as a single historical phenomenon, despite their formally disparate purposes and effects. Chapter 2 offers an account of the relationship of sovereignty and enclosure in modern political theory and opens up the predicament of power signified by eroding state sovereignty. Chapters 3 and 4 then develop the ways in which walls address the mutually imbricated threats to the identity and powers of states and subjects consequent to declining state sovereignty in late modernity. Chapter 3 focuses primarily on political examples and discourses for this work; Chapter 4 makes a turn to psychoanalysis.

Contemporary nation-state walling may be nameable as such, but does not emerge or appear in the world this way. With their distinctive political and economic contexts, varied histories, various stated purposes and effects, and disparate building materials and appearances, the new walls are not generally considered as a coherent or even common event. Thus, the claims I am forwarding assert connections among undertakings rarely recognized as kin.[10] What does it mean to treat nation-state walling as a theoretical object when it does not emerge and exist in the world as such?

Each of the new walls can be seen to issue from certain pressures on nations and states exerted by the process of globalization. All generate significant effects in excess of or even counter to their stated purposes; none really "work" in the sense of resolving or even substantially reducing the conflicts, hostilities, or traffic at which they officially aim; each is built as provisional while taking shape as permanent; and each is expensive, yet strikingly popular. These things can be said of every wall built by nation-states in the past two decades. Moreover, the walls themselves are increasingly linked by a diverse ensemble of circuitries, including border-fortification technologies, contractors and subcontractors, protest murals and graffiti, and, of course, legitimation. The global proliferation of walling itself increasingly legitimates walls, especially in Western democracies, where we would expect such legitimation to be hard won.

And yet, the differences among these barriers add up to an equally lengthy list. Some walls are little more than crude fences through fields, while others are mammoth, imposing structures heavily adorned with contemporary surveillance technology. They would also seem to address a diverse array of problems. Most South Asian nation-state walls, for example, target immigrants, while most of the walls of the Middle East are built in the name of security from terrorism. The Uzbekistan wall against Kyrgystan was prompted by border conflicts, while the Ceuta and Melilla walls in Morocco seek to prevent these Spanish enclaves from becoming staging grounds for Asians and Africans seeking to get to Europe. The berm across Morocco's Western Sahara aims to appropriate disputed territory and some also regard the Israeli wall as a land-grab.

Perhaps nowhere are these differences in purpose and effects sharper than in the two largest, most expensive, and most notorious of the new walls—Israel's "security fence" and the U.S. "border fence." The Israeli wall issues from the evolving architecture of settler colonialism and occupation. It constitutes a new strategy of separation in that context. The U.S. barrier responds mainly to U.S. popular anxieties about the effects of an impoverished Global South on the American economy and culture. Why and how to think about them together? Why harbor both under the aegis of eroding nation-state sovereignty in a post-Westphalian world?

The Israel Security Fence, a.k.a. "the Wall"

Sovereignty is at issue in a number of ways in the Israel-Palestinian conflict. There is the struggle for Palestinian sovereignty, the question of sovereign occupation, and the internally, mutually as well as internationally contested sovereignties of Israel and Palestine. There is also an open question about whether a political solution to the conflict would feature one or two sovereignties, perhaps even spatially overlapping sovereignties.[11] However, the global erosion of state sovereignty is not usually considered a factor driving the building of the Israeli wall in the West Bank. Like its predecessors on the Israeli and Egyptian borders of Gaza, the Wall is part of a specific development within the forty-year-old occupation of Palestine, a development broadly characterizable as a shift from colonial domination through administration and control of Palestinians to domination achieved through the

28

separation and deprivation of this population.[12] The barrier is one element in an arsenal of technologies and strategies for physically disentangling and spatially dividing two intimately entwined populations to create a future of what Prime Minister Ehud Barak defined pithily as "us here, them there."[13]

The Wall is simultaneously an architectural instrument of separation, of occupation, and of territorial expansion mandated by the twinning of state-sponsored and outlaw extensions of settler colonialism. As is well known, in the course of separating Palestine from Israel, the Wall responds as much to the problem of the Israeli settlements in the Occupied Palestinian Territories as to security threats posed by Palestinian terrorists or mass uprisings such as those of the two intifadas. While successive Israeli regimes overseeing the Wall's construction have determined to protect and incorporate the settlements, state sovereignty cannot be said to have established the historically contingent character of the Wall's jurisdiction, nor is the Wall ever officially defended as a sovereign jurisdictional border. Rather, it appears as a technology in a shifting state approach to a globally unique condition of mingled peoples, mangled sovereignties, colonial and anticolonial violence, appropriated and contested lands.

Given its singular context, multiple purposes, and the geographic, political, and military complexity of managing the occupation, what possible kinship does the Wall have with others around the globe? These affinities appear in some of its legitimation strategies, performances, and supplemental technologies, in its inconsistent textures, even in some of its effects and failures. If, for example, in certain places along its route, the Israeli barrier constitutes a technique of strategic land appropriation that poses as an antiterrorist technology, elsewhere, the Wall appears as an offensive political military technology, posing as a pacification structure, yet effecting economic disruption, social deracination, and psychic humiliation.[14] In places, the Wall produces garrisoned Israeli settlements akin to "gated communities" in the United States, except that, as land appropriations, these communities might be more appropriately compared to the Spanish enclaves in Morocco. In other places, the Wall segregates the ethnic quarters of Jerusalem, divides a university, cleaves a Palestinian town, family, orchard, or transportation route...ruptures and divisions that are repeated, sometimes lightly by comparison, at the sites of other walls. The Indo-Kashmir wall separates farmers from their lands. The U.S.-Mexico wall sunders a university in Brownsville, Texas, truncates family contact at the California and Arizona borders with Mexico, divides and desecrates Native American lands, and disrupts markets in labor and consumption long vital to communities on both sides of the border.[15]

But doesn't the purpose and trajectory of the Israeli wall remain singular? The Wall veers from the 1967 Green Line to wrap around settlements deep in the West Bank interior and includes a series of "depth barriers" accompanied by "sterile security zones" penetrating even further into Palestinian lands. These are among the features that make it not a mere border wall or security fence, but a technology of separation and domination in a complex context of settler colonialism and occupation. "The wall," Eyal Weizman writes, has "become a discontinuous and fragmented series of self-enclosed barriers that can be better understood as a prevalent 'condition' of segregation—a shifting frontier—rather than one continuous line cutting the territory in two."[16] It twists, turns, and frequently doubles back on itself as it wraps around hilltop settlements and divides Palestinian communities while establishing tiny strips of connection between pockets of Israeli Jewish existence in the West Bank. Also facilitating these connections across the field of separation is a growing network of roads and tunnels (respectively designated "Jewish" or "Palestinian," depending on what they connect and who has access to them) arching over and under the Wall and each other.

Still another feature of the Wall's seeming global uniqueness pertains to its temporally and spatially ad hoc and provisional qualities. Consequent to various constituencies that have shaped and reshaped its route, including the Israeli Supreme Court,

30 random
no structure

anti-Wall protestors, settlers, environmentalists, and realtors, the Wall's path has been repeatedly altered over the course of its construction. Moreover, it has never been formally anointed as a separation barrier, but rather has been built in the name of a "temporary" state of emergency constituted by Palestinian hostilities. It is officially declared removable and rerouteable as the security situation requires or as a political solution permits.[17] Critics Ariella Azoulay and Adi Ophir call this aspect of the Wall "a suspended political solution," cousin to the "suspended violence" they claim the Wall represents as it substitutes "insinuation and deterrence" for the material contact of conventional violence.[18] In addition to the abrogation or postponement of political agreements and settled sovereignties, the notion of "suspended political solutions" underscores the literal suspending of law, accountability, and legitimacy and the introduction of arbitrary and extralegal state prerogative that occurs in states of emergency. Thus, argue Azoulay and Ophir, "suspended violence in the territories preserves not the law but its very suspension, and it constitutes not a new law but a no-law situation...law has not been abolished altogether but merely suspended."[19] The invocation of an implicitly temporary "state of emergency" to legitimate lethal violence is not unique to the contemporary period in Israel, but is part of a larger and older discursive economy holding Palestinians responsible for soliciting each violent element in the Israeli arsenal and adducing reaction to these elements as justification for more Israeli violence. What is new is the paradox of the enormous and hugely expensive barrier in this context—the very building of which graphically challenges the idea of temporariness by which it is legitimated.

If the ad hoc and formally impermanent status of the Wall is sometimes part of its discursive legitimation, at other times, the Wall appears as a more straightforward border marker, an ordinary thing in an age of border walls and necessitated by ongoing hostilities. In Weizman's words, the wall "attempts to display the reassuring iconography of...a contiguous political border" even as it actually marks "the violent reality of a shifting colonial frontier. Notwithstanding the constant shifting of its route, in its massive physical presence that has made it the largest and most expensive project in the history of the state, the Wall seeks to appear as a heavily fortified border."[20]

Weizman's argument about the difference between barriers and borders is aimed at the specificity of the Israeli wall, but it is important for understanding many nation-state walls today. "Barriers," he writes, "do not separate the 'inside' of a sovereign, political or legal system from a foreign 'outside' but act as contingent structures to prevent movement across territory."[21] The Israeli wall is not unique in signifying alternately as barrier and border, sometimes fusing and sometimes separating the two, depending on legitimacy requirements or challenges. Most walls constructed by nation-states today draw on the easy legitimacy of sovereign border control even as they aim to function more as prophylactics against postnational, transnational, or subnational forces that do not align neatly with nation-states or their boundaries. Some therefore include variations on the Israeli "depth barrier," for example, the highway checkpoints fifteen miles north of the U.S. boundary with Mexico. Others appear as national boundary markers, but are actually driven by postnational investments in barriers to global immigration. Such is the case with the European Union contribution of more than 40 million Euros to fortify the Ceuta and Melilla walls in Morocco to deter Asian and African migration to Europe. The shifting fortification of Europe against immigration from the east, a task left to the easternmost nation recently added to the EU, is another instance of a postnational barrier appearing as a national border. Most walls continue to draw on the idea of nation-state sovereignty for their legitimacy *and* serve performatively to shore up nation-state sovereignty even as these barriers do not always conform to borders between nation-states and are themselves sometimes monuments to the fading strength or importance of nation-state sovereignty.

Moreover, notwithstanding their often exorbitant costs, elaborate theaters of construction, and significant effects on geopolitical and ecological landscapes, few of the recently constructed walls have been undertaken or promulgated as permanent. To the contrary, the model for legitimating the new walls is exemplified by the barricades composed of "Texas barriers" (outsized versions of the "Jersey barriers" conventionally used as roadblocks) planted around Baghdad in efforts to secure certain neighborhoods from sectarian violence. The walls come down when this violence provisionally recedes or relocates, a moment that the Western mainstream media often eagerly reports as a sign that the war and occupation are succeeding.[22] The putative impermanence of the new walls, their participation in the "suspended violence" legitimated by a state of emergency as theorized by Azoulay and Ophir, is of particular importance in liberal democracies, where walls risk offending whatever remains of commitments to universal inclusion and openness. Such commitments, of course, are fading. In the discourse of civilizational struggle that has superseded Cold War discourse in organizing the global imaginary of liberal democracies, two disparate images are merged to produce a single figure of danger justifying exclusion and closure: the hungry masses, on the one hand, and cultural-religious aggression toward Western values, on the other. This merging is abetted by the West's newly felt economic vulnerability to quarters of the world it has hitherto dominated or ignored. Civilizational discourse combined with this new economic landscape renders ever more acceptable to Western democrats the walling out of economic desperation *and* "foreign" or "inassimilable" cultures.[23]

In sum, while the Israeli wall has singular purposes and effects, many of its distinct features can be found in other walls in other parts of the world, although nowhere else in the same combination or with the same intensity of effects. If Israel's plight stems in part from having been established as a settler colony precisely when colonialism across the globe was being condemned and dismantled, if it is in this regard cursed by a globally rejected past in its present, Israel also seems to have the strange honor of honing the demographic and political-military tactics and technologies of the global future.[24] In this regard, the Israeli wall concentrates all the diverse performative functions, legitimating strategies, and technologies of modern spatial control, as well as all the contradictions found in contemporary walling projects. The Israeli wall, like the others, both performs and undoes a sovereign boundary function, just as it performs and undoes sovereign stability, legislative power, decisionism, and endurance. The Israeli wall, like the others, features a complicated dependence on an ideal of nation-state sovereignty whose very deterioration the Wall redresses, yet whose historical eclipse the Wall also consecrates. If the Wall is a bid for sovereignty, it is also a monstrous tribute to the waning viability of sovereign nation-states. From certain angles, it appears as an eerie monument to the impossibility of nation-state sovereignty today, even if there are unique dimensions to this impossibility in the Israel-Palestine context.

Other continuities between the Israeli barrier and those elsewhere in the world include the Wall's role in displacing Israeli domination onto the figure of a threatening and violent subordinate, its symbolic and psychological turning of the inside out. The Wall also shares with other walls the literal rerouting of danger that the wall purports to block, its intensification of enmity and incitement of new tactics and forms of aggression against what it would protect. It also shares the targeting of enemy populations not precisely commensurate with states or nations. And like all contemporary walls, the Wall generates (and sustains tensions between) theatrical, theological, and material effects.

Finally, it is important to note the policy architects of the Israeli wall legitimate it internationally both by claiming Israel is like other democracies that are fortifying their borders and through claims of Israeli exceptionalism. The Wall is built in the name of Israel's need to secure its population, as any "democracy" must, and also in the name of Israel's singular history and context. The Wall thus simultaneously places Israel in the company of civilized nations and speaks to its unique nature as a Jewish state surrounded by enemies. However, the discourses legitimating most nation-state walls today feature some version, even if a less dramatic one, of this Janus-faced positioning between the generic ("everyone is doing it") and the unique ("this is why *we* need this wall").

The U.S.-Mexico Border Barrier

Like the Israeli wall, at first blush, the U.S.-Mexico border barrier appears distinctive in purpose, function, and construction among the many walls being built around the world. Dividing the Global North from the Global South and aimed primarily at northward flows of illegal drugs and immigrants, it is a spectacularly large and expensive endeavor, one that also varies extensively along its route, ranging from sections that feature triply reinforced sixty-foot-high concrete and steel barriers, to lengths of "virtual fencing" composed of sensors, surveillance cameras, and other detection technology, to desert stretches consisting only of cement posts spaced to obstruct all-terrain vehicles.

The U.S. Border Patrol undertook the building of the first piece of the barrier, the "San Diego fence," in 1990. Extending from the Pacific Ocean fourteen miles inland and completed in 1993, the fence was constructed of air force landing mats remaindered from the Vietnam War, which turned out to be eminently climbable and lacked the visual awe of what was soon to come. In 1994, the Clinton administration launched Operation Gatekeeper to supply additional fortification and enforcement resources to this part of the border, the main effect of which was to reduce crossings and crime in the urban areas while driving immigration eastward and bulking up the smuggling industry. Operation Hold the Line and Operation Safeguard, established at the major crossing points in Arizona and Texas (and extended into New Mexico), had similar effects. However, as popular sentiment quickened for "doing something" about illegal immigration, politicians across the political spectrum vied with each other for reputations of

35

toughness on the border. Meanwhile, as neoliberalization stripped protections from North American producers and proliferated global production of cheap goods and services, U.S. employers (especially, but not only in agriculture and construction) relied ever more heavily and openly on illegal immigrant labor. Thus, the walling project was born out of a tension between the needs of North American capital and popular antagonism toward the migration incited by those needs, especially their effect on wages, employment, and the demographics and cultures composing and in some eyes decomposing the nation.

In 1996, Congress passed the Illegal Immigration Reform and Immigrant Responsibility Act to authorize an extension of the U.S.-Mexico barrier and a secondary layer of fencing and security roads intended to buttress ineffective primary fencing. However, environmental challenges raised by the California Coastal Commission and uncooperative owners of property abutting the border soon stalled construction. These and other legal challenges were eventually overcome by the 2005 Real ID Act and the 2006 Secure Fence Act, which rode the wave of post-9/11 security concerns to waive impeding laws and require the construction of 850 miles of fencing in five separate stretches of the Mexico border with California, Arizona, and Texas. The Real ID Act has broad scope, authorizing the waiver of *all* legal impediments to the construction of the barrier and permitting judicial review only for constitutional claims.[25] To date, thirty-six laws have been set aside in the course of construction, including statutes concerned with water and air pollution, endangered species protection, animal migration, historic preservation, farmland protection, and Native American sacred lands provisions. In setting aside such legal statutes, these two acts situate the U.S. walling project as a response to a "state of emergency," bidding to protect a vulnerable nation under siege and relating it to the "suspended political solution" orchestrating the building of the Israeli wall.

Sentiment about the border fence runs high in American politics, both for and against, although those in favor have the ears of

36

the mainstream media and politicians. Support for the barrier in communities nearest the border is surprisingly weak; proximity tends to breed greater appreciation of its limited effectiveness in stemming as opposed to rerouting illegal immigration, and border communities are also where economic interdependence with Mexico may be most deeply felt.[26] That said, there is still plenty of organized support for the wall in border states, areas that are also home to the vigilante groups devoted to patrolling the border and hunting down illegal crossers.

The cost of the wall is difficult to establish. Much federal expenditure of bureaucratic and manual labor related to planning, building, maintaining, and analyzing the effectiveness of the wall is excluded from calculations. Predictions and budgets for the barrier have also varied substantially over the two decades of its emergence, and the estimates still range widely, both for original construction and for maintenance and repair over time. More of the construction has been outsourced to private contractors than was originally planned, and early estimates of sections priced at $3 million per mile have come in at as much as seven times that. Excluding the costs of land acquisition and labor, the Army Corps of Engineers now predicts that the twenty-five-year life-cycle cost of the 850-mile barrier mandated by the Secure Fence Act will range from $16.4 million to $70 million per mile, depending on the nature of the barricade in various areas and on the amount of damage it sustains from smugglers.[27] Completion and maintenance of the barrier mandated by the act could cost up to $60 *billion* over twenty-five years, a figure that excludes federally funded labor and remuneration to private-property holders whose land is used for fencing or patrolling the barrier.

What makes these figures even more remarkable is the limited effectiveness of the barrier in actually deterring, as opposed to rerouting, the flow of illegal immigration. Proclamations of the wall's "success" refer only to reduced illegal crossings and apprehensions in urban areas and not to illegal immigration and drug smuggling rates as a whole.[28] While it is easier for the

37

Border Patrol to catch illegal border crossers in open areas than in urban ones, where they can quickly disappear into neighborhoods, mountain, desert, sea, and tunnel smuggling operations have grown more sophisticated in response to the barrier. These operations and the counterresponses by the Border Patrol in turn increase the general level and geographical reach of violence and criminality at the border, including in previously peaceful remote regions.[29] Moreover, by shifting migration to more geographically challenging areas, the barrier has dramatically increased both migrant deaths and the rate of permanent, rather than temporary migration into the United States.

What ever they are try to stop by pussing or borders is increasing other problems

In short, the U.S.-Mexico barrier stages a sovereign power and control that it does not exercise, is built from the fabric of a suspended rule of law and fiscal nonaccountability, has multiplied and intensified criminal industries, and is an icon of the combination of sovereign erosion and heightened xenophobia and nationalism increasingly prevalent in Western democracies today. The state of emergency out of which the wall's construction is authorized also gives it political standing independent of its material functions.

While the Israeli wall issues from and deepens contradictions generated for sovereignty by expansionist colonial occupation, the U.S. barrier issues from and deepens contradictions generated for First World sovereign integrity and capacity by neoliberal globalization. The walls respond to and externalize the causes of different kinds of perceived violence to the nation, and the walls themselves exercise different kinds of violence toward the families, communities, livelihoods, lands, and political possibilities they traverse and shape. However, both are ultimately ineffective bulwarks against the pressures and violences generated in part by the power and resources of the political entities building them. Both are nonetheless extremely popular. Both intensify the criminality and violence they purport to repel, and hence, both generate the need for more fortifications and policing. Yet both are heralded for producing peace, order, and security. Both stage a sovereignty that the barriers themselves undermine. Both mobilize sovereign jurisdictionality, both confound barricades and borders, and both articulate a border on confiscated lands. Both walled democracies are justified as state necessity in protecting the people, both draw upon the xenophobia they also exacerbate and project, both suspend the law in the name of blockading outlaws and criminals, and both build a "suspended political solution" in concrete and barbed wire. In sum, the differences between the new walls matter, but should not blind us to the shared predicaments of power they respond to and articulate.

If there are common fields and predicaments of power generating diversely placed and purposed new walls, are there also continuities between the new walls and their many predecessors in history? This book argues for a post-Westphalian distinctiveness to contemporary walls, a distinctiveness inhering in the reaction they represent to the dissolving effects of globalization on nation-state sovereignty. This distinctiveness appears in the fact the new walls are built to blockade flows of people, contraband, and violence that do not emanate from sovereign entities and in the fact that they perform an increasingly troubled and unviable sovereign state power. The new walls iterate, in this regard, a vanishing political imaginary in a global interregnum, a time after the era of state sovereignty, but before the articulation or instantiation of an alternate global order.

But there have been political walls before. Indeed, there have been fences since the Beginning, and despite the new walls' distinctive global context, there exist certain continuities between contemporary walls and older walls. Political walls have always spectacularized power — they have always generated performative and symbolic effects in excess of their obdurately material ones. They have produced and negated certain political imaginaries. They have contributed to the political subjectivity of those they encompass and those they exclude. Medieval walls and fortresses dotting the European countryside, for example, officially built against invasion, also served to overawe and hence bind and pacify

What the book is about

the towns they encircled.[30] More generally, all walls defining or defending political entities have shaped collective and individual identity within as they aimed to block penetration from without. This is as true of the Great Wall of China as of contemporary gated communities in the U.S. Southwest. Even the infamous walling projects of twentieth-century Europe combined these functions and effects. The Maginot Line, which stood for the defense of France's eastern border against German invasion, was conceived to produce the image of an "impenetrable fortress France," yet was never intended to be built *in toto*. The rhetoric of the wall vastly outran the bits and pieces of its construction.[31] The Atlantik Wall built by the Third Reich against an anticipated Allied invasion launched from Great Britain was also designed as a graphic symbol of Nazi-controlled Europe. The Berlin Wall, retrospectively signifying the imprisonment of a population presumed desirous of escaping Soviet domination, was originally conceived as a protective cordon around a fragile new society, a society based on work, cooperation, and egalitarianism, rather than individualism, competition, and hierarchy. The architects of the new Communist society believed the laboratory of social and psychological experiments out of which it would be born required insulation from a corrupting and decadent outside.[32]

Like the Berlin Wall, contemporary walls, especially those around democracies, often undo or invert the contrasts they are meant to inscribe. Officially aimed at protecting putatively free, open, lawful, and secular societies from trespass, exploitation, or attack, the walls are built of suspended law and inadvertently produce a collective ethos and subjectivity that is defensive, parochial, nationalistic, and militarized. They generate an increasingly closed and policed collective identity in place of the open society they would defend. Thus, the new walls are not merely ineffective in resurrecting the eroding nation-state sovereignty to which they respond, but they contribute new forms of xenophobia and parochialism to a postnational era. They abet the production of subjects defended against worldliness, but also, ironically,

40

subjects who lack the very sovereign capaciousness that walled democracy would protect as its prize.

German historian Greg Eghigian has given the name "homo munitus" to the conformist, passive, paranoid, and predictable creature that is the walled nation or subject.[33] Drawing on the Latin *munire*, which means to fortify, secure, defend, protect, or shelter, Eghigian examines both Western mythology and the actual production of East German subjectivity behind the Berlin Wall. While contesting the Western (liberal democratic) norm by which this subjectivity is measured, he corroborates the popular image of the personality produced by the wall, an image that comports in striking ways with Western contemporary imaginings of obeisant and deindividuated theocratic subjects cast as the enemy or at least the opposite of Western individuals.[34] Thus, the kinds of subjects that Western nation-state walls would block out are paradoxically produced within by the walls themselves—yet another way in which walls inadvertently subvert the distinction between inside and outside that they are intended to mark, a distinction also underscored by contemporary walling advocates eager to disassociate our walls from the Berlin Wall or to distinguish between walls that limn free and unfree societies.

The recognition that walls do not merely protect but produce the content of the nations they barricade permits us to ask not only what psychological needs and desires fuel their construction, but what contingent effects they have in contouring nationalisms, citizen subjectivities, and identities of the political entities on both of their sides. It permits us to consider whether and how contemporary walls work as symbols of collective and individual containment, as fortifications for entities whose real and imagined borders globalization places under erasure. It allows us to ask whether they are containing as well as defending, indeed, whether all defense entails containment and all containment entails defense. When do the new walls become like the confining walls of a prison, rather than the comforting walls of a house? When does the fortress become a penitentiary?

During the Cold War, the Euro-Atlantic left posed this question routinely about the civil defense shelters touted by Western political and civic leaders as vital in the contest between East and West. The shelters, even unused, contributed to a widespread bunker mentality amid the nuclear arms build-up, a mentality that itself reinforced rather than questioned the assumptions and strategies undergirding American defense and foreign policy in the 1950s and 1960s. Stockpiled nuclear weapons in bunkered silos were mirrored by stockpiled subsistence supplies in bunkered shelters; defending against Armageddon became a mutually reinforcing way of civilian and political life, one that also obscured the American contribution to this deadly standoff. Left Israelis today pose a similar question as the project of walling in West Bank and Gaza residents not only decreases the possibilities for a political solution, but intensifies the militarization and bunker mentality contouring Israeli life.

Walls built around political entities cannot block out without shutting in, cannot secure without making securitization a way of life, cannot define an external "they" without producing a reactionary "we," even as they also undermine the basis of that distinction. Psychically, socially, and politically, walls inevitably convert a protected way of life into hunkering and huddling. In this respect, the Berlin Wall, whose tearing down twenty years ago is still internationally celebrated and whose imprisoning functions are contrasted by contemporary walling advocates with the task of protecting free societies, is not quite so opposite to twenty-first-century walls as such advocates would suggest.

42

CHAPTER TWO

Sovereignty and Enclosure

Every new age and every new epoch in the coexistence of peoples, empires and countries, of rulers and power formations of every sort, is founded on new spatial divisions, new enclosures, and new spatial orders of the earth.
—Carl Schmitt, *Nomos of the Earth*

Pale: 1) picket or stake for a fence; 2) space or field having bounds; enclosure; a territory or district under a certain jurisdiction; 3) an area or the limits within which one is privileged or protected.
—*Merriam-Webster's Dictionary*

"In the beginning was the fence," writes Jost Trier. "The enclosure gave birth to the shrine by removing it from the ordinary, placing it under its own laws, and entrusting it to the divine."[1] And just as enclosure lies at the origin of the sacred, it also marks out the beginning of the secular: "The first person who, having fenced off a plot of ground, took it into his head to say *this is mine* and found people simple enough to believe him, was the true founder of civil society," Rousseau insists in his "Discourse on Inequality."[2]

"In the beginning was the fence," but also in the end? Perhaps what Rousseau describes as the territorial *mine* inaugurating civil society and what Trier accounts as the sacred dimension of enclosure together not only found political sovereignty, but reappear at the moment of political sovereignty's dissipation or transformation. Thus would the walling of the nation-state be the death

43

rattle of landed nation-state sovereignty, possibly even signifying a certain theological remainder in its wake.[3]

John Locke is the early modern theorist who articulates most directly the role of land appropriation in political founding *and* in relating the sovereignty of states and individuals. The *Second Treatise on Government* features bounded proprietorship as the pivot that, through the vehicle of tacit consent derived from inheritance, secures and reproduces the relationship of individual and state sovereignty. Obtaining legal status and protection for property ownership motivates entry into the social contract, while political power itself is defined as "a right of making laws...for the regulating and preserving of property."[4] Carl Schmitt, then, exaggerates only slightly in *Nomos of the Earth* when he says that for Locke, "the essence of political power is its jurisdiction over the land."[5] Fences, titles, and enclosures are among Locke's most fecund and ubiquitous metaphors in the *Second Treatise*; they secure freedom, representation, and limits to the right of rebellion, as well as actual territory. Conversely, Locke argues, it is partly for lack of clear and settled dominion over land that "Indians in America" cannot be said to enjoy political sovereignty and thereby remain in a state of political savagery.[6] *meaning act of violent cruelty*

The property-minded Locke is only one of the most explicit in linking land appropriation, enclosure, ownership and the founding of sovereign power and right. As Schmitt writes, early modern political theorists from Vico to Kant (and, I would add, from Machiavelli to Rousseau) formulated land appropriation as the foundation of political sovereignty and the essential precondition for public and private law, ownership, and order. For Schmitt, "land appropriation is the primary legal title that underlies all subsequent law." It "constitutes the original spatial order, the source of all further concrete order and all further law." It is "the reproductive root in the normative order of history."[7]

We have ceased to appreciate the importance of this origin, Schmitt argues, in part because we have lost the "energy and majesty" of the word *nomos*, a word now conventionally translated as

44

"law," "regulation," or "norm," but that Schmitt claims was originally and fundamentally a *spatial* term. *Nomos* expresses the production of (political) order through spatial orientation. The word
nomos derives from *nemein*, Schmitt reminds us, which means
both "to divide" and "to pasture." Thus, *nomos* "is the immediate
form in which the political and social order of a people becomes
spatially visible." Drawing on Trier's analyses of the primeval
ritual of making an enclosing ring out of men's bodies (the "manring"), Schmitt insists that all "law and peace originally rested on
enclosures in the spatial sense" and that "every nomos consists of
what is within its own bounds." Thus, he concludes, "*nomos* can
be described as a wall," and "like a wall it, too, is based on sacred
orientations."[8] There is first the enclosure and then the sovereign.
Or, put the other way around, it is through the walling off of
space from the common that sovereignty is born.

Schmitt's etymology of *nomos* may be contested, and his emphasis on land appropriation as the essential foundation of all order may
be overstated, but his appreciation of enclosure as a prerequisite
of political order and law is difficult to set aside.[9] This prerequisite could even constitute a fundamental challenge for advocates of global citizenship or democracy without borders: How
is an unbounded polity possible? The line is the basis of constitu-
tion, of *pouvoir constitué* within what it encloses, as well as the
threshold beyond which the law does not hold. "Beyond the line,"
Schmitt says, force can be used "freely and ruthlessly," with indifference to law.[10] Hence the layers of meaning and history packed
into the expression "beyond the pale," a phrase conjuring what
lies outside the bounds of "propriety and courtesy" but also of
"protection and safety."[11] The boundary designated by a pale—
a wooden stake used to make a fence—originally delineated English
colonial territory in Ireland. Tellingly, this colonial territory itself
came to be called "The Pale." With Schmitt's formulation of the
relation of fencing to *nomos* as our guide, what is "beyond the pale"
appears as uncivilized in two disparate, yet politically linked senses:
It is where civilization ends, but it is also where the brutishness of

45

the civilized is therefore permitted, where violence may be freely and legitimately exercised. Compressed into this phrase is thus a historical-ontological circuitry linking the staking out of a settler colony by the British, the British colonial view of the Irish as uncivilized, and therefore the legitimacy of British violence toward the Irish, that is, justification of both the original colonial conquest and the continued use of violence in defending the colony. This discursive circuitry is repeated in encounters declared "outside the pale" of civilization today, whether in Gaza, Kabul, or Guantánamo.

"Every *nomos* consists of what is within its own bounds," Schmitt writes. A state of exception—the declaring of "martial law"—is precisely the suspension of law in time and space. It eliminates the boundary between inside and outside, permitting the indifference to the law that is normally reserved for the outside to come inside. This is also how *nomos* organizes space in time: "*Nomos* is a matter of the fundamental process of apportioning space essential to every historical epoch, a matter of the structure-determining convergence of order and orientation in the cohabitation of peoples on this...planet."[12]

Although he does not pursue it, Schmitt draws our attention to another crucial feature of the work of demarcation through fencing, namely, its relation to the sacred—its immediate association of the political with the theological. Not only is "*nomos*...like a wall...based on sacred orientation," but "all human *nomoi* are nourished by a single divine *nomos*."[13] The shrine is always enclosed or encircled, whether with elaborate temples or with stones simply, yet deliberately laid out in a forest or pasture. The enclosure brings the sacred into being, marking it off from the common or the ordinary. Thus, the medieval city walls whose ruins still litter European soil may have functioned as protection, but were performatively and symbolically most important in marking off the city from the vast space of the countryside. Never only a means of walling out, these walls served to bound, establish, and consecrate the entity dominating the surrounding countryside.[14] Like the walls of houses, but also and importantly

46

like the walls of temples, the city walls produced a legal and political entity upon which they also conferred a sacred quality. What may appear as tautological in Schmitt's claims—that sovereignty is originally theological and that enclosure generates both sovereignty and the sacred—is resolved as the coconstitutive relation of sovereignty, theology, and enclosure. The fence founds and relates sacred space and sovereign power. We should therefore not be surprised to discover a theological aspect in late modern walling projects, one whispering the decline of nation-state sovereignty.

Founded through enclosure, dominion and jurisdiction soon become premises of sovereignty, even its presuppositions, rather than marks of its essential attributes. None of the great theorists of sovereignty identify it with the power to *designate* dominion, but instead with absolute power over this dominion. Sovereignty is identified with settled jurisdiction, not with settling it. Put the other way around, land jurisdiction premises rather than constitutes earthly sovereignty for the classical theorists. And even its part in founding recedes as the increased size of political entities requires that political sovereignty, like the nation itself, comes to have an ever greater *imagined* dimension. The relative diminution of agriculture in political economy also alters the status of land in the lexicon of political power, and technological developments in warfare eliminate territorial jurisdiction as the sole or even major plane of confrontation between sovereigns. Walls never wholly disappear from the geopolitical map, and walling projects, mostly undertaken in either the anticipation or the aftermath of great wars, remain important tablets of world history. Still, in modernity, the idea of physically enclosing geopolitical entities became exceptional, rather than normal, reserved mainly for colonial outposts in hostile territory or for delineating Cold War boundaries such as those in Germany, Korea, and Hong Kong.

Sovereignty, Enclosure, and Democracy
We speak of sovereignty today as if we know what we mean when we discuss its existence, achievement, violation, assertion,

jurisdiction, or even waning. Yet sovereignty is an unusually amorphous, elusive, and polysemic term of political life. George W. Bush was not alone in defining it tautologically: "sovereignty means…you've been given sovereignty…and you're viewed as a sovereign entity."[15] Its primordial status as "the unmoved mover" is often noted in contemporary scholarly discussions.[16] Even among political theorists, sovereignty is used in a variety of different and underspecified ways. For some, it is equated with the rule and jurisdiction of law and for others with legitimate extralegal action, just as some insist on its inherently absolute and unified nature, while others insist that it can be both partial and divisible.[17]

To a degree, political sovereignty's roving and ambiguous meaning today derives from its peculiar double place in liberal democracy and the shell game with power that this double place facilitates in liberal democratic practice, where what denotes sovereignty in the Schmittian sense (decisionist state power) is not named as sovereign in the Lockean or Rousseauian sense (popular legislative power). The premise of democracy is that sovereignty lies with the people, yet liberalism also necessarily features what Locke names "prerogative power"—the power of the executive to abrogate or suspend the law or to act without regard for the law—and it is the latter that critical theorists and commentators have in mind when they object to dangerous or excessive sovereign power today.[18] Contemporary theoretical discussions of sovereignty in democracies tend to be centered upon the state's power to act without regard for law or legitimacy, rather than upon the power of the *demos* to make laws for itself, a slip that either outs liberalism as tacitly conferring sovereignty to nonrepresentative state power while denying that it does so or suggests the extent to which the Schmittian intellectual revival has overwhelmed contemporary discussions of sovereignty.[19]

Let us consider more closely the difficulty of thinking about sovereignty from the vantage point of liberal democracy, especially at this historical moment. The relationship between

48

democracy and sovereignty is posed as a question today consequent to the partial and uneven deconstitution of the sovereign nation-state in late modernity, a deconstitution effected by unprecedented flows of economic, moral, political, and theological power across national boundaries. It is a question posed as well by the overtly imperial conduct, during the Cold War and also in its aftermath, of the world's oldest continuous democracy, the legitimating aim of which, universal democracy, has paradoxically entailed both domestic subversions of democracy and disregard for other nation-state sovereignties. It is a question posed, too, by the ongoing occupation of Iraq, in which the twin policy aims of installing managed (market) democracy and producing Iraqi sovereignty appear only vaguely linked and both of which are seriously stalled. And it is a question posed by the evolution of the European Union as postnational political forms intersect with transnational economic powers to foment a panoply of anxieties among Europeans about the means by which democracy can be secured and practiced.

But even prior to this set of recent historical conundrums, the sovereignty-democracy relation was a puzzle. If "popular sovereignty" has tripped easily off the tongues of Westerners for three centuries, it remains one of the more strikingly catachrestic terms to enter ordinary discourse in the era of nation-states, and Kant is not the only thinker claimed by contemporary liberals to have declared it an "absurdity."[20] It is nearly impossible to reconcile the classical features of sovereignty—power that is not only foundational and unimpeachable, but enduring and indivisible, magisterial and awe-inducing, decisive and supralegal—with the requisites of rule by the *demos*. Again, the very fact that the people are declared sovereign in Western democracies while the appellation of sovereign power is given to autocratic state action and especially to action that violates or suspends democratic principles suggests that we have known all along that popular sovereignty has been, if not a fiction, something of an abstraction with a tenuous bearing on political reality. What, otherwise, does it mean to identify as sovereign those state acts that suspend or abridge the very rule of law that signifies democracy, or to speak, as we often do today, of expanded executive or state powers in terms of resurging or expanding sovereign power?

From a slightly different angle, sovereignty in liberal democracy can be seen to work in a double register, one of routine legitimacy, law, and elections and another of state action or decisionism. What we call the state in liberal democracies comprises both, which is why Locke subdivided the powers of the state, yet formulated prerogative power (state sovereignty) as precisely what can suspend or set aside legislative power (popular sovereignty).[21] Locke softened the appearance of this move by defining prerogative power as "nothing but the Power of doing publick good without a Rule," but knew this power is uniquely vulnerable to getting out of hand: Excess in its use was the sole justification Locke offered for a people's exercise of the right of revolution.[22] More important for our purposes, insofar as the people authorize the suspension of their own legislative power in granting prerogative power to the executive, they suspend their sovereignty in the name of their own protection or need. But a sovereign that suspends its sovereignty is no sovereign. Thus does Locke's thought grow incoherent in a way avoided by Hobbes.

More generally, the problem with formulating sovereignty as divided, separated, or disseminated is the incompatibility of this move with an irreducible feature of sovereignty—not its unconditioned, a priori or unitary aspects, but its finality and decisiveness.[23] It is these last qualities that make sovereignty something that either is or is not. There can be no "sort of" sovereign, any more than there can be a "sort of" God, and as the current predicament of Iraq attests, the idea of partial or provisional sovereignty is worse than unstable and incoherent. Nor, conventionally, can there be multiple sovereigns in a single jurisdiction or entity. Historically, sovereignty has delineated political identity through jurisdiction.[24]

Indeed, it is precisely over colliding sovereign claims that wars are fought, lawsuits are filed, religions do battle (with each other or with states), and human beings psychologically disintegrate. If, as Schmitt suggests, political sovereignty derives its shape and power from God, it does more than episodically trump the power or authority or legitimacy of laws and elections and more than stand as the symbolic origin of them. It is final and absolute, hence indivisible and nontransferable. It cannot circulate, cede, delegate, or self-suspend any more than divine power can. If the people are sovereign, if this is the meaning of *cracy* by the *demos*, then their shared power must be decisive, in which case a sovereign state cannot suspend this power. Conversely, where sovereignty rests with the state or an executive, democracy does not actually prevail. The "rule of the people" becomes at best a discontinuous, episodic, and subordinate *practice*, rather than an actual sovereign power.[25] If, on the other hand, sovereignty is separated from rule, if the people are only episodically decisive (every four or six years), then rule is not a form of self-determination, and sovereignty is not a form of rule.

The incoherent splitting of sovereignty between the people and the state in liberal democracy is the contradiction at the heart of this political form that is seized upon by Rousseau in *The Social Contract* and also pursued relentlessly by Marx in "On the Jewish Question." The very existence of the state as what overcomes our particularity and, in Hegel's words, realizes our freedom is evidence for Marx that we do not actually rule ourselves or live freely. If we did, the state would not be required for this overcoming and realization. Yet—and here is where we no sooner pick up Marx than leave him again—it would also seem there can be no political life without sovereignty, that is, without decisiveness and finality and above all without a power that gathers, mobilizes, and deploys the collective force of an entity on behalf of and against itself, as both its means of governing and its means of ordering itself. Not by itself and yet essentially, sovereignty gives and represents political form. Sovereignty is inherently antidemocratic insofar as it must overcome the dispersed quality of power in a democracy, but democracy, to be politically viable, to be a (political) contender, appears to require the supplement of sovereignty. Derrida affirms this paradox in his passing remark in *Rogues*, "it is not certain that 'democracy' is a political concept through and through."[26]

Sovereignty as/at the Border

Apart from the distinctive problematic of sovereignty's place in democracy, there is ambiguity in the term and paradox in the phenomenon itself. Sovereignty is a peculiar border concept,[27] not only demarking the boundaries of an entity, but through this demarcation setting terms and organizing the space both inside and outside the entity. As a boundary marker that is also a form of power, sovereignty bears two different faces. These appear in two different dictionary meanings of "sovereignty," "supremacy" and "autonomy," and two equally discrepant political usages, as decisive power or rule and as freedom from occupation by another.[28] Within the space that is its jurisdiction, sovereignty signifies supremacy of power or authority (a meaning also captured by the Middle English use of the term for a husband or master, as in "my sovereign, my lord"). Yet turned outward, or in the space beyond its jurisdiction, sovereignty conveys self-rule and the capacity for independence in action. Inside, sovereignty expresses power beyond accountability. Outside, sovereignty expresses the capacity for autonomous agency, including aggression or defense against other sovereign entities.[29] The two usages are related, of course, insofar as it is the supremacy within that enables the autonomy without. The autonomy derives from the convening and mobilizing by a master power of an otherwise diffuse body—whether a diverse population or the diverse inclinations of an individual subject. The importance of sovereignty's attributes of unity and indivisibility, then, is that they literally enable the autonomy that is its external sign. Sovereignty does not simply unify or repress its subjects, but is rather both generated by and generative of these subjects. It promises to convene and mobilize the energies of a body to render it capable of autonomous action.

This is one reason why Schmitt formulates *order* as a crucial effect and accomplishment of sovereignty.[30]

(Liberalism seeks to split the supremacy from the autonomy, the power of the people from the action of the state. But as already suggested, in so doing, liberalism disavows the nonsupremacy of the *demos* at the moment of sovereign state action and makes sovereignty itself incoherent. It disavows the inherently antidemocratic moment in the production of state autonomy and the incoherence for popular sovereignty that results. This is the incoherence of submitting autonomy to the rule of law and of generating an autonomous power out of a state designed to secure individual rights. Moreover, insofar as internal and external dangers are what activate the state, when these dangers become persistent or permanent, the outside turns inward, taking the form of lawless autonomous action directed toward the populace, unifying this populace through an act of subordination by which sovereignty itself is produced. Hegel discerned and distilled this incoherence in his discussion of popular sovereignty in the *Philosophy of Right*.)[31]

There are a number of paradoxes of sovereignty that are subsets of its Janus-faced character, its different meaning and operations within and without.

1. Sovereignty is both a name for absolute power and a name for political freedom.

2. Sovereignty generates order through subordination and freedom through autonomy.

3. Sovereignty has no internal essence, but rather is completely dependent and relational, even as it stands for autonomy, self-presence, and self-sufficiency.[32]

4. Sovereignty produces both internal hierarchy (sovereignty is always sovereignty over something) and external anarchy (by definition, there can be nothing governing a sovereign entity, so if there is more than one sovereign entity in the universe, there is necessarily anarchy among them). Importantly, both hierarchy and anarchy are at odds with democracy, if the latter

is understood as a modestly egalitarian sharing of power. Yet with rare exceptions, political theorists take sovereignty to be a necessary feature of political life: The very possibility of political action, political order, and political protection seem to depend upon it. Perhaps the existence of this paradox is one reason why liberals tend not to examine sovereignty closely, even as they assume that it rests with the people, but also why radicals such as Giorgio Agamben, Michael Hardt, and Antonio Negri develop a politics opposed to sovereignty and why leftish liberals such as William Connolly seek to pluralize and disseminate sovereignty's undemocratic core.[33]

5. Sovereignty is both a sign of the rule and jurisdiction of law and supervenes the law. Or sovereignty is both the source of law and above the law, the origin of juridicism and what resides outside it. It is all law and no law. Its every utterance is law, and it is lawless.

6. Sovereignty is also both generated and generative, yet it is also ontologically a priori, presupposed, original. Even practically, as Jean Bodin notes, sovereignty cannot be conferred.[34] The presupposed or a priori nature of political sovereignty is both drawn from theology and is part of what gives sovereignty religious dimensions. It is a reminder that all political sovereignty is modeled on that religiously attributed to God.

7. The theological aspect of sovereignty is the internal condition of the secular notion of the autonomy of the political articulated by and through sovereignty. As the next section will suggest, this paradox is particularly important to grasping what is becoming of political sovereignty today.[35]

Sovereign Autonomy and the Autonomy of the Political

Carl Schmitt is the thinker who explicitly crafts the concept of the autonomy of the political through the concept of sovereignty. Schmitt famously identifies the political with the friend-enemy distinction "as the utmost degree of intensity of a union or disassociation."[36] This identification in turn generates the signature action of political life, *deciding* who the enemy is and what to do about the enmity. Decisionism, in turn, is the defining action and expression of sovereignty: "sovereign is he who decides on the exception."[37] And response to the friend-enemy condition—a response that can neither be codified nor normalized—is the defining action of the political. Political action that breaks with the norm also happens to be what breaks apart the liberal equation of the political and the juridical.

Decisionism, which Schmitt defines as "pure will that bows before no sovereign truth," is *the* modality of political action because the political itself is sovereign, subject neither to norms nor to law, accountable to nothing else and derived from nothing else.[38] The sovereignty of the political proceeds from its purview over the life-and-death matter of the friend-enemy relation and more precisely from two facts: On the one hand, life is at stake, while on the other, there can be no norm to decide on or about the enemy. Nor is there just a missing rule or convention here. Rather, this decision is "beyond the pale" and necessarily rests outside whatever norms bind the polity, even as it may pertain to protecting the way of life these norms govern and bind.

If the decision about who the enemy is and what to do about it is *the* political decision, and if the autonomous capacity to make these decisions is the sign of political sovereignty, then sovereignty in turn articulates a certain autonomy of the political. This line of reasoning, congealed as a thesis, is generally regarded as the heart of Schmitt's antiliberalism. It is the basis of Schmitt's critique of a liberal foregrounding of law, norm, and procedure in politics. For Schmitt, this foregrounding compromises the political insofar as it compromises its autonomy and hence its sovereignty.[39]

Most liberal democrats regard Schmitt's thesis as shocking and unacceptable. But to the extent that a softened version of it appears in social contract theory, Schmitt may be more of a bold messenger than an iconoclast here. In contrast with Aristotle's notion that political life is natural to man, indeed, that the *polis* is man's distinct "life form," in social contract theory, the political emerges from a nonpolitical ontological condition and is brought into being through artifice. The birth of the political through the social contract is, at the same time, the birth of political sovereignty. The social contract constitutes the temporal end and spatial limit of the sovereignty of nature or God and the inauguration of a distinctly human form in the domain of the political. The contract simultaneously establishes the sovereignty and the autonomy of the political, even if the subjective motivations for entering into the social contract are social or economic, for example, the desire for security in life, liberty, property, or possessions or the desire to resolve or temper the despotism of nature. The social contract is precisely what separates out and establishes the autonomy and sovereignty of the political at the same time that it establishes political sovereignty. As apparent in the harsh authoritarianism of Hobbes as it is in the soft liberalism of Mill, and made explicit by the social contract stories of Rousseau and Locke, the jurisdiction of the political is distinct from those of nature, God, and family and is suppose to facilitate and contain economic life.[40]

What are the implications of sovereignty signifying both the autonomy of a polity and the autonomy of the political? As we have already learned, the two-sided nature of sovereignty means that its external autonomy entails internal mastery or subordination of powers that would rival, disperse, or fragment it. Thus, the autonomy of the political articulated by sovereignty entails the conceit of the political dominance or containment of other powers, including the economic and the religious. Political sovereignty by definition subtends these other powers. In this regard, sovereignty represents both a cleansing or purification of the political and the supreme reign of the political. Again, this is a purification and reign that is extremely consequential, despite being aspirational, ideological, even mythical, rather than literal.

Through the classic works of early modernity and their contextualization in bloody religious wars, we are attuned to the quest for mastery over transnational religious authority sought by political sovereignty attached to nation-states. Equally important, however, is political sovereignty's bid to subordinate the economic to the political. This is not to say that the modern sovereign nation-state always heavy-handedly governs or regulates the economy, but that it is premised on the notion that it can and that it *decides* whether and when to do so. Laissez-faire capitalism is as much the expression of such a decision as is New Deal monetary and fiscal policy or state socialism.

Political sovereignty's reach for autonomy from/mastery over the economic is well captured in an anachronistic meaning of "sovereign" as the gold coin (also known as the "coin of the realm") minted in England from the time of Henry VII to that of Charles I and introduced to replace local and ad hoc currencies. The identification of currency with the Crown ("crown" also being another name for the coin) signifies a subtending of the economic by the political and, more specifically, the Crown's assertion of political control over the economy in order to unify and consolidate the realm. This meaning suggests as well that sovereignty is never simply held and wielded, but from the beginning *circulates*—it works as currency and through currency, and not only through law or command.[41] (Just as sovereignty takes over theological practices of power, including making its word into law, it takes over economic practices of power, including circulation, fetishism, incorporation, and more.) The generation of a coin of the realm in the early seventeenth century, like the generation of the euro four centuries later, reminds us that the early modern preoccupation with sovereignty coincides with both the consolidation of nation-state sovereignty out of decentralized local, political, and economic powers (the abolition of local currencies aims to abolish local sovereignties) and an anxious response to the emergent force of capital in mercantile economies, a force that would burst national boundaries of wealth accumulation and circulation as it internationalized markets and production. So sovereignty here expresses the subordination of the economic to the political, paradoxically, but unsurprisingly at the very moment when the economic was evincing its own power and its resistance to such subordination.[42]

This thesis about the relation of political sovereignty to the economic differs from that put forth by Hardt and Negri, for whom sovereignty emerges in service to the economic. Capital, they claim in *Empire*, becomes the content of the political form of sovereignty.[43] By contrast, I am arguing that even if the modern state emerges and develops, inter alia, in response to capital, political sovereignty — as idea, fiction, or practice — is neither equivalent to the state nor merely in the service of capital. Rather, sovereignty is a *theological* political formulation and formation that aims, inter alia, to subordinate and contain the economic and to detach political life from the demands or imperatives of the economic. That this aspiration is ultimately unrealizable does not prevent it from becoming a potent material fiction with significant effects during its reign. Neither political nor economic practice bear the substantive distinctiveness implied by political sovereignty invested in nation-states, but both have been shaped historically by this investment.

The Theology of Sovereignty

Just as the early modern emergence of political sovereignty responded to political economy's power in social or political life by attempting both to contain and to co-opt this power, it did something similar with religion. The context of the early modern religious wars produced state sovereignty as both a reaction against religious authority and an attempt to appropriate it. This reaction and appropriation is apparent in political sovereignty's God-like characteristics. Ontologically, sovereignty is the unmoved mover. Epistemologically, it is a priori. As a power, it is supreme, unified, unaccountable, and generative. It is the source, condition, and protector of civic life and a unique form of power insofar as it brings a new entity into being and sustains control over its creation. It punishes *and* protects. It is the source of law and above the law.

58

[handwritten marginal note: action of taking something for one's own use w/o permission]

The homological and isomorphic dimensions of the relation between political sovereignty and God are not merely the result of reactive imitation or appropriation. God is the original sovereign and is overtly displaced by political sovereignty in early modern theoretical accounts. But more than its origin, the theological remains a necessary supplement to political sovereignty, making political sovereignty work yet not made manifest in its workings. Why? "All significant concepts of the modern theory of the state are secularized theological concepts," writes Schmitt, because these concepts were literally borrowed from theology, because of their systematic structure, and because of the state's status as an "invisible person."[44] Again, however, this thesis is not unique to Schmitt. There is Hobbes's infamous opening of *Leviathan*: "Nature (the art whereby God hath made and governs the world) is by the art of man, as in many other things, so in this also imitated."[45] Leviathan, the literally terrifying monster made by God, is imitated, rivaled, and finally bested by the issue of man's own creative powers.[46] Or in a softer reading of Hobbes, if God makes man, man makes the larger and more powerful collective subject that is the commonwealth.

Sovereignty, Hobbes writes in the Introduction to *Leviathan*, is the soul of this man-made creature. Sovereignty "gives life and motion to the whole body."[47] Consider the implications of designating sovereignty as the soul of the commonwealth. First, it is a life principle, that which animates and governs the movements of the commonwealth, and not simply a politically repressive solution to civil strife or external danger. Second, sovereignty, though made by human artifice, is linked to God; souls are the sign of God's presence in earthly bodies—they come from God and return to God. Thus Hobbes does not simply rival God but instrumentalizes him in constructing political sovereignty, an instrumentalization that is repeated in Parts 3 and 4 of *Leviathan*, where Hobbes both establishes the consonance between Christianity and the commonwealth, and mobilizes the fear of God to produce fealty to the commonwealth. Perhaps most importantly,

59

feelings ≈
admiration
fear or
wonder

Hobbes describes both God and sovereignty as powers that overawe; sovereignty literally imitates God's induction of awe in
subjects, not merely his power. Or, political sovereignty is the
power-form that works by overawing us, rather than by governance or rule.[48] The borrowing from God here is complex. By
analogizing sovereignty to the soul of the "Artificial Man" generated by human artifice, Hobbes reveals a fundamental trick of
sovereignty: We generate and authorize what then overawes us
and is unaccountable to us because of its divine status. Man generates political sovereignty through the conferral of his own power,
but since sovereignty is the divine element within the commonwealth, this process of generation or fabrication is disavowed and
covered over.

Just as Hobbes's account of political sovereignty borrows
explicitly from God for its power and legitimacy, has recourse to
God for sanctification of its status, and as "soul" is the token or
presence of God in the commonwealth, there are similar links
between political and divine sovereignty in other early modern
theories of sovereignty, including those of Abbé Sieyès, Jean
Bodin, and Jean-Jacques Rousseau. Moreover, the divine quality of political sovereignty is what articulates the fiction of its
containment of economic powers. In *What is the Third Estate?* for
example, Abbé Sieyès makes clear that while political economy
is what generates the social contract, political sovereignty is its
effect. Thus, in his brief for radical popular sovereignty, Sieyès literally theorizes the subordination of the economic by the political
as the logic and the conclusion of the social contract. But this
logic depends upon a theological rendering of the political will of
the nation as a priori, eternal, the foundation of all law and existing prior to the law.[49]

For Jean Bodin, the identification of political sovereignty with
God is in part a technique for containing potential excesses or
abuses of sovereignty. When Bodin says "justice is the end of
the law, law the work of the prince, and the prince the image of
God. Hence, the law of the prince must be modeled on the law

60

of God,"[50] he draws a set of links between God and sovereign political power that simultaneously produce the absolutism of sovereignty and hedge sovereign power with God's own law and beneficence. Sovereign power, supreme on earth, at once imitates God and becomes something like a mediator for God. As I will suggest toward the end of this chapter, if Bodin's hope was to limit abuses by linking political sovereignty with God, today, this same link may license rather than contain aspiring sovereigns who cast themselves as mediators for God or in the service of God—whether Allah, Jahweh, or the Christian Lord.

The persistent theological dimension of sovereignty is even evident in the respective religious modalities through which contemporary theorists conceive sovereignty. Think of Agamben's formalistic account, in which sovereignty and *homo sacer* are as timeless and eternal as the Latin Mass. Or of Connolly's (still theological) atheism, which attempts to withdraw omnipotence, supreme power, and totality from the concept of sovereignty, insisting instead on its porous, layered, oscillating, and pluralizable character, even making it quotidian, rather than awe-inducing and otherworldly. Or consider Foucault, the lapsed Catholic, for whom sovereignty is mostly a story we tell ourselves, one that shrouds the real story, yet is nearly impossible to escape and that also provides a certain comfort. Or think of Hardt and Negri, for whom sovereignty only and always suppresses the multitude and must be opposed, as God must be, for the multitude to know and enact its own messianic powers. The point is that even at the theoretical level, political sovereignty is never without theological structure and overtones, whether it is impersonating, dispelling, killing, rivaling, or serving God. But the containment and regulation of religion is also always a dimension of political sovereignty's function, even in the most overtly religious or theocratic states. And because its own power derives in part from appropriating and imitating what it neuters and subtends, political sovereignty is not undone by refusing to believe in God or by the death of God.

61

The Late Modern Waning of Political Sovereignty and the Decontainment of Religion and Capital

If political sovereignty is structured theologically as the supreme and unaccountable political power and draws on God for legitimacy, and if its theological dimensions enable the conceit of the autonomy and sovereignty of the political vis-à-vis the economic, what happens as nation-state sovereignty wanes? What becomes of the theology of the autonomy of the political in the post-Westphalian era? What transformation of political sovereignty and state power is consequent to the transnational flows of capital, labor, people, ideas, cultures, and religious and political fealties that erode political sovereignty from inside and outside nation-states? My speculative theses are these: As it is weakened and rivaled by other forces, what remains of nation-state sovereignty becomes openly and aggressively rather than passively theological. So also do popular desires for restored sovereign might and protection carry a strongly religious aura. At the same time, declining nation-state sovereignty decontains theological and economic powers, a decontainment that itself abets the erosion of nation-state sovereignty.

Theological Political Sovereignty

As nation-state sovereignty wanes, both internal and external performances of it are increasingly and openly dressed in religious regalia. Countless activations of political power today rest on a strange brew of gratifying the will of Allah, Jahweh, or a New Testament God, on the one hand, and fulfilling vaguely liberal democratic principles, on the other. While, for example, President George W. Bush yoked American imperial actions to the delivery of the Almighty's "gift of freedom," the Iranian president elected in June 2005 declared Iranians to be as free as Allah intended and linked his renewed nuclear weapons program to the service of Allah.[51] President Obama cited the "special relationship" between the United States and Israel as deriving from the latter's status as "an independent Jewish state" and "the

62

used god as inspiration or in support of god

only true democracy in the Middle East."[52] Bush invoked God
to legitimate his use of veto powers or proposed constitutional
amendments to protect "unborn life" (from abortion) and the
"sanctity of marriage" (from homosexuals) inside the United
States and to withdraw funds from organizations promoting con-
dom use or abortifacients in other nations. Obama also cites
his religious beliefs as the basis of his opposition to same-sex
marriage, although he has not overtly mobilized state power on
this issue. As these invocations are paralleled by state and stateless sovereigns resting their authority with other gods, Samuel
Huntington's much-derided thesis of civilizational clash takes
on a different hue: Conflicting sovereign and would-be sovereign powers in late modernity appear to serve warring godheads (Christian, Muslim, Jewish, Hindu, or other), even if these
godheads do not align precisely with nation-states and hence
with the political sovereignties of the Westphalian period. That
is, although there are religious states, the state is not the only
or even primary agent of religiously legitimated violence today.
Rather, as waning nation-state sovereignty decontains religious
power, that power takes up residence in a variety of more and
less violent subnational or postnational constellations. At the
same time, however, this makes national and even state religion appear less strange than it would otherwise in a putatively
secular age.

From a different angle, political sovereignty's theological
dimension becomes more manifest as nation-state sovereignty
itself weakens. Concretely, sovereignty needs God more as its
other sources and powers thin and its territorial grip falters.
(Religion has also intensified as a critical link between national
and transnational fealties in the post-Westphalian era, not only
for Muslims and Jews, but also for Christians, even as the link for
Christians often takes the form of "defending the West" against
the rest.) In a historical twist of fate, this reemergence of the
theological face of late modern sovereignty makes Israel's forthrightly religious national identity and justifications for violence,

not to mention its walls, less anomalous than they might have been 50 or 100 years ago.

The Decontainment of Religion and the Waning of Sovereignty

In the course of its waning, nation-state sovereignty becomes more intensively and openly theological, but this contributes to its undoing in the long run. On the one hand, the religions that sovereignty mobilizes are transnational, rather than national, and hence contribute to the erosion of nation-state sovereignty that prompts its theological outing in the first place. On the other hand, interpretations and implications of these religions vary even within national settings, and religion is as likely to instrumentalize the nation-state as the other way around. From the mosque movement in Egypt to rapture Christians and AIPAC in the United States, from the scarf affair in France to the threat of civil war from orthodox settlers in Israel, from rising Islam in secular Turkey to the militancy of the Falun Gong in China, sovereign states are newly vulnerable to politicized religious claims, transnational religious forces, religious conflict, and unmanageable cultural and religious heterogeneities in the nations for whose unification and protection they stand.

Capital

While local (statist, substatist, and transnational) bursts of political sovereignty cloak themselves in God talk and are asserted through demands for fealty and claims to paternalistic protection in an openly theological frame, capital takes shape as an emerging *global* sovereign. Capital alone appears perpetual and absolute, increasingly unaccountable and primordial, the source of all commands, yet beyond the reach of the *nomos*. Capital produces life absent provisions of protection and ties of membership, turning populations around the world into *homo sacer*.[53] Yet capital also links the diverse peoples and cultures of the world, supplanting other forms of association with its own. Capital creates the conditions (or their absence) for all sentient life while

64

being fully accountable to no political sovereign. Capital mocks efforts by national and subnational communities to contour their ways of life or to direct their own fates, making such efforts appear similar to those of feudal fiefdoms at the dawn of modernity. And neoliberal political rationality, which disseminates market rationality across the social and governmental fields, is itself a prescription for and endorsement of capital as would-be global sovereign.[54]

However, although capitalist managers certainly decide things, the sovereign action of capital does not take the form of decisionism and is not centered on the friend-enemy relation, which means that capital lacks both the purview and the signature that Schmitt attributed to political sovereignty. If global capital is perpetual, absolute, and unifying, but is not political or decisionist in the Schmittian sense, it would seem that rather than being relocated *in toto*, there is a dissemination of elements of political sovereignty in the post-Westphalian period. Capital appears to be ascending to a form of sovereignty without a sovereign, that is, without an anthropomorphized God at its heart. At first blush, this would seem to comport with a view of capital as a relentless force of desacralization, a view proffered by both Marxists and neoliberals, who regard the market as attenuating religious and tribal passions and attachments.[55] But there is another way to understand global capital as embodying elements of sovereignty without the sovereign. Perhaps it is in a certain way more God-like than modern political sovereigns ever were, insofar as it more closely approximates a god's power to make the world without deliberation or calculation. Decisionism, which connotes choice, knowledge, judgment, even doubt and uncertainty, may then turn out to be the first human form of sovereignty, the one carrying an Aristotelian appreciation of the political as the distinctly human thing and of humans as distinctively political. This means that the Schmittian definition of sovereign as "he who decides" would pertain only when "he" is human, rather than divine—it would pertain only to *political* sovereignty. This alternative reading turns the first one inside out: as capital, God is not dead, but rather finally deanthropomorphized—finally God.

Here is how the theses concerning the unleashing of religious power and the sovereignty of global capital could be put together: Capital is both master and coin of the realm, except there is no realm, no global polity, governance, or society, and neither are there boundaries or territory that delimit capital's domain. Rather, today, we face increasingly faltering theological political sovereignty, on the one hand, and capital as global power, on the other. This makes for a strange inversion and paradox. While weakening nation-state sovereigns yoke their fate and legitimacy to God, capital, that most desacralizing of forces, becomes God-like: almighty, limitless, and uncontrollable. In what should be the final and complete triumph of secularism, there is only theology. This is how the post-Westphalian decontainment of the theological and the economic rhetorically echo each other, even as they move along distinct trajectories.

States without Sovereignty

To this point we have mainly followed sovereignty's course in the contemporary coming apart of sovereignty and nation-states. Let us turn now to the other part of the constellation: What are the implications for state action and state power of this coming apart? In *Losing Control?* Saskia Sassen argues that globalization "has entailed a partial denationalization of national territory and partial shift of some components of state sovereignty to other institutions, from supranational entities to the global capital market."[56] This shift does not mean that states have ceased to be important and powerful world actors. Rather, as Sassen insists, the role and status of states in both domestic and international politics have been altered by the twin forces of denationalized economic space and renationalized political discourse, by the separation of sovereignty from states.[57]

This alteration, I would argue, complicates Derrida's suggestion that there are rogue states as soon as there are sovereign states, that sovereignty, insofar as it operates apart from the law, generates and licenses roguishness.[58] Derrida's Schmittian insight is technically correct, but in a post-Westphalian epoch, another kind of state roguishness appears in global and domestic politics, one that emanates from states increasingly losing their grip on sovereign power. As I suggested at the beginning of the chapter, such rogue-state behavior—manifest, inter alia, in the building of walls—may look like hypersovereignty, but is actually often compensating for its loss. Lacking sovereign supremacy and majesty, yet invoking sovereign prerogative and guile, postsovereign states become peculiar new kinds of international actors.

The posturing and hyperbole that result constitute only one feature of late modern states without sovereignty. States remain important global actors in world markets, in the moral-political discourse of international human rights, and in a variety of international and transnational relations governed by Realpolitik.[59] The fall 2008 finance capital meltdown made obvious to any who doubted it the extent to which states remain vital in stabilizing markets and facilitating conditions of capital accumulation. However, far from instancing state sovereignty, this activity revealed the degree of state subordination to capital. Indeed, states' status as neoliberal actors—and as neoliberalized (or in Foucault's lexicon, "governmentalized") themselves—is one index of their loss of political sovereignty. States do not dominate or order, but react to the movements and imperatives of capital as well as to other global phenomena, ranging from climate change to transnational terror networks. They cannot long pursue parochial or short-run national interests without worsening their positions. The autonomy of the political constitutive of the concept of political sovereignty has thus ceased to be an operative or convincing fiction.

Yet states remain a, if not the crucial emblem of political belonging and political protection. The plight of refugees and other stateless peoples is a reminder of the extent to which states remain the only meaningful sites of political citizenship and rights guarantees, as well as the most enduring emblems of

security, however thin practices of citizenship have become, however compromised and unevenly distributed rights may be, even
in democracies, however scored with fault lines is the *patria*'s
protective capacity, and however important postnational constellations of governance such as the European Union have become.
Hannah Arendt's account of the predicament of postwar stateless peoples, originally formulated as part of a critique of state
sovereignty, remains equally relevant to the period of political
sovereignty's decline and dissemination:

> The calamity of the rightless is not that they are deprived of life,
> liberty and the pursuit of happiness, or of equality before the law
> and freedom of opinion — formulas which were designed to solve
> problems within given communities — but they no longer belong
> to any community whatsoever. Their plight is not that they are not
> equal before the law but that no law exists for them; not that they
> are oppressed but that nobody wants even to oppress them.[60]

In their combined activities of supporting global markets and
conferring belonging and protection to subjects, states today
mediate tensions between global economic life and national political life. They are crucial regulators, owners, consumers, and sup-
pliers of capital, labor, resources, and goods, and they also work
to offset the sometimes deleterious effects of globalization on the
integrity of national political life. More than merely cleaning up
after the domestic human and environmental damage done by
capitalist production, as they did at the height of welfare state
capitalism, all states increasingly shoulder the task of protecting
national populations against the ravaging effects of open markets
on everything, including the national imaginary.[61]

A number of domestic political issues take shape at the nexus
of what Sassen terms "denationalized economic life and renationalized political life," including those concerned with labor,
agriculture, manufacturing, energy, and the environment.[62] Each
of these generates calls for national preferences that chafe against
free-market contexts. However, almost nothing rivals the image

of immigrant hordes as an incitement to xenophobic nationalism and to demands for fierce state protectionism amid globalization. Or perhaps there is now a rival for this position in the figure of the terrorist. If open borders are (falsely) held responsible for growing refugee and immigrant populations and border fortifications are (falsely) imagined capable of stemming this tide, porous borders are also commonly figured as the scrim through which terror slips. The two dangers, of course, are frequently twinned in the figure of the Arab Muslim. No matter that the vast majority of terror episodes in the United States have been homegrown, carried out by white male citizens and aimed at the state by the heartland, and that the guns and explosives used in these attacks are also sourced domestically. No matter that border fortifications can have little or no effect on the most dangerous instruments of terror—biological and nuclear weapons or hijacked airplanes. The call for states to close and secure national borders is fueled by populations anxious about everything from their physical security and economic well-being to their psychic sense of "I" and "we." Today, xenophobia is so overdetermined by the economic and political insecurities generated by globalization that even politicians cognizant of the limited efficacy of border fortifications lack discursive points of entry for discussing them.

Sovereign Decline and the Theology of Walling

Political sovereignty has always been something of a fiction, especially in democracies, where sovereignty slides between popular and absolutist formulations, hence between an abstraction that invests sovereignty in the people and an abrogation of democracy that invests it in autonomous state power. The detachment of sovereign power from the state in late modernity reveals this fiction more readily, which does not mean that states are finished as powerful actors, only as sovereign ones. This disestablishment of political sovereignty, however, creates more than a technical shift in orders and fields of power. It generates a potential political-theological crisis, one that ramifies from subject to state and one

69

to which the building of walls responds. Offering the spectacle of a clear and strong inside/outside, friend/enemy distinction comporting (or aiming to comport) with national borders, the new nation-state walls are iconographic of sovereign land enclosure and sovereign powers of protection and containment in the face of the dissolution of these powers.

The state can be divided, disunified, subordinated, even captured, and still survive. Not so *political* sovereignty, which, like God, is finished as soon as it is broken apart. Political sovereignty may be a secularized theological concept, but secularization, we need remember, does not mean the end of religion. Rather, secularization produces religion without the sword, religion located and deployed apart from direct political authority.[63] This means that sovereignty secularized for political purposes does not lose its religious structure or bearing, even as it ceases to have the direct authority of God at its heart. As "secular" political authority is substituted for God's, the religious modality of the authority persists. Paradoxically, religion indirectly recovers its sword as it reemerges in the form of political sovereignty.

Put slightly differently, whether it is understood to rest in the people or in a monarch, whether it is identified with the rule of law, the rule of the demos, or the chief executive of the nation, political sovereignty sustains a historical, performative, and rhetorical link with God and a significant reliance on a religious modality of belief and recognition. For Schmitt, political sovereignty's most important theological religious trace materializes in the exception, "analogous to the miracle in theology"; for Hobbes, this trace is to be found in sovereign subjects' absolute submission, obeisance, and awe; and for Bodin, it lies in reverence: "Contempt for one's sovereign prince is contempt toward God, of whom he is the earthly image."[64]

Political sovereignty's necessary entailment of the autonomy and supremacy of the political is also a remnant of this origin. The idea of political sovereignty depends on the conceit that political life dominates other fields of power and activity, including those conventionally named the social, economic, religious, and cultural. If political power is not sovereign over these fields, if it cannot deal with them decisively when necessary (in the moment of the exception), then political sovereignty cannot be said to exist. It would remain vulnerable to these other fields of power, contestable and potentially manipulable by them, and hence, not sovereign. Thus do Schmitt's formulations of sovereignty and the political depend upon each other, and thus does the idea of political sovereignty replicate the conceit of God's dominion over all, or as Bodin has it, political sovereignty "imitates" religious sovereignty. In the same vein, a sacred emanation is a crucial constitutive dimension of sovereignty, and awe is a crucial effect. *Majestas*, Derrida reminds us, "has always been a synonym of sovereignty."[65]

A wide range of thinkers—Dostoyevsky, Freud, Feuerbach, Nietzsche—suggest that the very idea of religious sovereignty, of a supreme, infinite, and supervenient power, is born of the human experience of smallness and vulnerability in a huge and overwhelming universe and that it harbors a desire for protection, containment, and orientation in the face of this experience. Political sovereignty, too, provides horizons and compass points for knowing and belonging and carries as well the promise of protection. What becomes of the wish for these things when political sovereignty erodes, the predicament in which nations and their inhabitants find themselves today? Walls signify, inter alia, desires for containment and security, responding especially to the powers that declining political sovereignty has unleashed, those of capital and religiously legitimated violence. It is these powers that produce the paradoxical splitting of sovereignty and fencing in our time. On the one hand, there is sovereignty after the fence, sovereign powers (capital, religiously sanctioned violence) without specified jurisdiction or enclosure and without even the promise of containment or protection. On the other, there is fencing after sovereignty, nation-states lacking sovereign powers to delimit and secure their territories and populations.

CHAPTER THREE

States and Subjects

Myth conflates with the propaganda; the rampart is also ideological, serving both to reassure the population and to disarm the adversary with a sense of the invincible, the impregnable.... The last citadel is a theater where wars past and present concentrate themselves.... The intense propaganda around the construction of the Second World War's fortifications (the Maginot Line as well as the Atlantic Wall) reveals their theatrics, their necessarily spectacular side.
—Paul Virilio, *Bunker Archeology*

A Common-wealth, without Sovereign Power, is but a word, without substance, and cannot stand.
—Thomas Hobbes, *Leviathan*

However architecturally interesting or complex, walls are conventionally regarded as functional instruments for dividing, separating, retaining, protecting, shoring up, or supporting. Whether constructing a building, holding back land erosion, or limning neighborhoods, walls are ordinarily perceived as intended for a material task. Yet walls are also commonly said to convey moods or feelings by their design, placement, and relationship to built or natural environments. They may set or foreclose political and economic possibilities and be screens for a host of projected desires, needs, or anxieties. In this respect, walls can be crucial elements in the making of what Edward Said termed "imaginative geography," the mental organization of space producing identities

73

through boundaries: "A group of people living on a few acres of land will set up boundaries between their land and...the territory beyond, which they call 'the land of the barbarians.'" This "imaginative geography of the 'our land—barbarian land' variety does not require that the barbarians acknowledge the distinction. It is enough for 'us' to set these boundaries in our own minds; 'they' become 'they' accordingly."[1]

Two commonplaces, then: Walls are consummately functional, and walls are potent organizers of human psychic landscapes generative of cultural and political identities. Here is how these might be put together: A wall as such has no intrinsic or persistent meaning or signification. As social theorist Paul Hirst insists, buildings do not narrate and are not themselves narratives.[2] Buildings are not "texts or pictures," philosopher Nelson Goodman adds, and do not "describe, recount, depict or portray. They mean, if at all, in other ways."[3] Thus, while the Wailing Wall may be the most sacred site on earth for religious Jews, the Great Wall of China carries a thousand years of South Asian history, and the wall of the Vietnam War Memorial in Washington, D.C. is unparalleled in its capacity to evoke memory and reckoning with that particularly dark hour in American foreign policy, walls as such do not tell a story. They emerge from and figure in discourses, they can become discursive statements themselves, and they are crucial to the organization of power in and through space. Walls may be said to be ugly, sad, imposing, comforting, magnificent, beautiful, and even righteous or unjust, but these judgments are not equivalent to intrinsic or timeless meanings or based on narratives resting in walls themselves. The meaning is not in the referent. Walls do not narrate and do not even speak.

Perhaps this is why Said turns to poetics in his own discussion of the spatial imaginaries produced by boundaries and structures. Borrowing from French philosopher Gaston Bachelard's *Poetics of Space*, Said writes:

> The objective space of a house—its corners, corridors, cellar, rooms—is far less important than what poetically it is endowed with,

74

which is usually a quality with an imaginative or figurative value we can name and feel: thus a house may be haunted, or homelike, or prisonlike or magical. So space acquires emotion and even rational sense by a kind of poetic process, whereby the vacant or anonymous reaches of distance are converted into meaning for us here.[4]

In addition to poetic associations and histories attached to built structures, and in addition to the discourses through which we understand them, context is of special importance in how we perceive and experience walls. Consider, for example, how differently two identical walls would "read" if one is built to shield a neighborhood from the sights and sounds of a freeway and the other to divide a white neighborhood in Italy from the streets on which recent immigrants have settled. There are differences even before we introduce the important question of who is doing the reading—the urban dweller screened from highway noise or a passerby whose home has not been so protected, the old European or a recent arrival from North Africa. Or consider the difference in the way the black granite wall of the Vietnam War Memorial in Washington, D.C., was understood by its designer—"I had an impulse to cut open the earth...an initial violence that in time would heal. The grass would grow back but the cut would remain...like a geode when you cut into it and polish the earth"—and by some war veterans and others who initially protested the design: "A black gash of shame...a tombstone... a wailing wall for draft dodgers and New Lefters of the future... a monument to defeat."[5] Consider even how differently a gated community appears when it is an anomaly in an otherwise open city versus when it is one among dozens organizing an American suburb or when it is situated in Southern California versus war-torn Baghdad.

Walls and other fortifications may also signify differently at different times of their lives: The Great Wall of China is a reminder of this, as is the Atlantik Wall built by the Nazis. In an extended essay on the latter, whose ruins served as a playground in his youth, Paul Virilio writes:

The poetry of the bunker is in its still being a shield for its users, in the end as outdated as an infant's rebuilt armor, an empty shell, an emotionally moving phantom of an old-fashioned duel in which the adversaries could still look each other in the eye through the narrow slits of their helmets. The bunker is the protohistory of an age in which the power of a single weapon is so great that no distance can protect you from it any longer.... Abandoned on the sand of the littoral like the skin of a species that has disappeared, the bunker is the last theatrical gesture in the end game of Occidental military history.[6]

If the discourses through which walls signify and are interpreted shift over time, they are also multiple and inconstant across the subjects they organize and the regional locales they may traverse. It is too simple, for example, to say that the Israeli wall connotes protection and security to one side and aggression, violation, and domination to the other. While the Wall may comport with an entitlement to safety in a Jewish homeland felt by some Israeli Jews, it carries for others the shame and violence of the occupation. Moreover, these discourses will continue to undergo temporal and spatial shifts, altering over the years of the Wall's existence and with its changing effects on the spaces and peoples it cleaves, traverses, produces.

Another example of the complex relation of physical structures and the temporality of discourses imbuing them with meaning can be found in post-9/11 security architecture in the United States. In the aftermath of the terrorist attacks on New York and Washington, hundreds of "Jersey barriers" (those familiar "upside-down T" temporary cement roadblocks, so named because they were first used in the building of the New Jersey Turnpike) were installed around federal buildings and the White House in Washington, D.C., and in the Wall Street section of New York City. The barriers would be mainly effective as protection against suicide car bombers, weapons that had no part in the events of 9/11 in the United States or in other events of the time, such as the anthrax attacks the following month or even in the Tokyo sarin nerve gas attack half a decade earlier. Nor were suicide car bombs among the weapons of mass destruction about which the Department of Homeland Security or the State Department had grown most concerned in the immediate aftermath of 9/11. Why, then, the Jersey barriers? Architectural scholar Trevor Boddy names their use in this period "fear theming," and situates them as part of an "architecture of disassurance" helping to produce the visual scenography of a state of emergency.[7] Given the mood of the day, the barriers worked performatively in a manner similar to hyper-vigilant inspections of baby strollers at airport security stations. Irrelevant to intercepting national security threats, they were consequential in inducing and sustaining a sense of imminent or proximate danger, which in turn eased the way for any state measure, from undertaking invasions to suspending constitutional provisions, allied with protecting the nation.

By late 2004, however, the Jersey barriers scattered around downtown Washington and the New York financial district had been removed. Again, why? According to Boddy, it was not because worries about terrorism had passed, but because of an altered public national security discourse. Washington's National Capital Planning Commission had come to worry that the barriers were "communicating fear and retrenchment, and undermin[ing] the basic premises of an open and democratic society."[8] Eventually, this architecture of disassurance was replaced with an architecture of security that was visible without being scarring, blending much more smoothly into an upscale urban contemporary aesthetic. The new architecture included structures such as the "NOGO barrier" (structurally adaptable and moveable impact posts placed in sidewalks and driveways) and the "Tiger Trap" (surfaces that can support pedestrians, but fall away under vehicle weight, trapping any wayward vehicle below ground).[9] More than a replacement of temporary with permanent structures, these installations signaled a changing discourse about fear, danger, and nation, one that shifted from an image of the United States as a wounded giant hunkered down against frightening attacks of

77

unknown origin and magnitude to one depicting it as master of security—smooth, confident, prepared.

Appreciation of the ways in which walls operate within the contextual and discursive frames of meanings generating and generated by the built environment underlines the importance of grasping the contexts in which the new walls are being built. This book does not explore those contexts in their national particularity—someone should—but rather in the larger historically specific context of declining state sovereignty. Emphasis upon the context generating the material and psychological meaning and effects of walls also suggests the importance of considering nation-state walling from the perspective of subjects, as well as states, that is, from the perspective of political desire, as well as that of political power, and in terms of the nexus of symbolic and affective representations and appeals that inflect both and join the two together. These two registers, of course, are not fully separable, and there is no sharp distinction between popular and more official political discourses generating the demand for walling, legitimating walling, or construing its meaning. State legitimacy often turns on addressing social desires that do not comport with state interests. Conversely, subjects do not always want what the state may require, for example, war or taxes, even as they may be drawn into or mobilized by these requirements. As the post-9/11 Jersey barrier story suggests, state-generated discourses of fear and danger reflect, interpellate, and construct the affect of subjects. On the other hand, the discrepancy between intense popular agitation for a barrier along the southern border of the United States and dubiousness about its efficacy by most policy analysts is a reminder that state aims are necessarily shaped and constrained by popular desires and fantasies.

State policies and subject desires are difficult to disentangle in another sense. While the same forces of globalization challenge the sovereignty of both subject and state, liberal discourse also links eroded state sovereignty with the endangered sovereignty of the subject. Transgressed and unprotectable political boundaries are the undoing of both. Moreover, subjects may sometimes identify with or as state sovereignty, and the state in turn may be identified with or as a vulnerable subject in need of protection. This projective identification is facilitated in liberal democracies by what was introduced in Chapter 2 as the circuitry between state and individual sovereignty at the heart of the liberal social contract. From Hobbes to Locke, from Rousseau to Hegel, political sovereignty is taken to secure and enlarge the social sovereignty of the subject. A certain primitive individual sovereignty is assumed in the state of nature, of course, but it is a sovereignty so fragile and insecure, so vulnerable to injury, enslavement, or death, so unable to enlarge its purview through property and possessions, that it can be understood only as a kind of antitheological sovereignty. That is, this primitive individual sovereignty is the literal inverse of political sovereignty formulated as a secularized version of God's unlimited power and through which human beings are protected. Man prior to the state is rendered by liberal discourse, especially its Hobbesian variant, not as having great powers and jurisdiction, but as relentlessly imperiled and reactive, living in "continual fear and danger of violent death" and unable to accomplish or protect much of anything in life.[10] Within a liberal ontology, the decline of state sovereignty therefore threatens a return to an intensely vulnerable and violable condition of existence for subjects.

In view of the several levels of intimacy and identification between state and individual sovereignty and the ways in which walls themselves are sites of mobilizations between state and subject, discussions of the two cannot be cleanly separated. This chapter considers the intersections of state and subject motivations, as well as the mutual imbrication of material and subjective forces that together generate the frenzy of wall building today. The next chapter probes in more explicitly psychological terms the production of vulnerable and unprotected late modern subjects desirous of walled nation-states.

Sovereign Failure

What is striking about the walls proliferating at the dawn of the twenty-first century is their seemingly physical, obdurate, premodern signature in the context of a late modern world in which power is networked, virtual, microphysical, even liquid, and peoples are increasingly linked, if not hybridized. However accustomed we have grown to checkpointed thresholds striating everyday life—at the entrances of museums, concerts, sports events, schools, airports—there is a markedly archaic quality to the slow and manifest construction of walls fashioned from concrete, brick, iron, steel, barbed wire, or even synthetic mesh. Compared with the evanescent, protean, and depthless traits of late modern culture and politics, walls seem solid and permanent, and appear to lack capacities for guile and dissimulation. (The nomenclature, of course, often aims to dissimulate—the Israeli "security fence," the U.S. "border marker," the Northern Irish "peace lines"—but such nomenclature is openly mocked by the unmaskable characteristics of the referent and by the protest murals and graffiti often adorning that referent.)[11] While we navigate scores of virtual walls every day—firewalls, spyware and spam filters on our computers, automatic locking and alarm systems in cars, homes, office buildings, and briefcases, pass codes everywhere—the spectacle of these actual walls remains distinctive. Their physicality makes them seem like a literal throwback to another time, a time of fortresses and kings, militias and moats, Guelphs and Ghibellines, rather than a time of smart bombs, missile shields in space, global warming, digital touch pads, and peoples and dangers so literally on the move and so radically miscegenated as to be no more containable by a physical land barrier than is air pollution or a new strain of influenza.

Moreover, contemporary critical theory has attuned us to modalities of power radically at odds with either the symbolic or literal prophylactic of walls. We have learned, especially from late twentieth-century Continental thought, to keep our eye on power's discursive dross, its noncentralized habitus, its noncommodifiable operation and its deterritorialization. Jacques Derrida alerts us to power's residence and operation in language, Michel de Certeau to power's spatial mobility, Michel Foucault and Gilles Deleuze to its disciplinary or networked qualities, its rhizomatic, irrigating, or circulatory movements, its light and vaporous qualities even as it orchestrates unprecedented effects of domination. Still others have illuminated power's location in culture, symbolic orders, psyches, science, and a panoply of other knowledges. By contrast, walls appear to harken back to a modality and ontology of power that is sovereign, spatially bounded, and territorial. Walls would seem to express power that is material, visible, centralized, and exerted corporeally through overt force and policing. *Pace* Foucault's critique of the "repressive hypothesis" and emphasis on the productive, rather than the repressive or censorious aspects of power, walls would seem to embody precisely the power of the "no," physically proclaiming and enforcing what is *interdit*. The new walls thus seem to stand as a certain kind of rebuke to every poststructuralist theorization of power as well as to every liberal hope for a global village. Indeed, as the walls limning nations and high-security prisons come increasingly to resemble one another and to share technology and construction outfits, not only does a regime of disciplinary power seem to fade before one of an older carcerality, the promise of a globally connected human world, one bathed in liberal freedoms, is contravened by one in which cement, barbed wire, checkpoints, and surveillance appear the norm.

The relation of nation-state walls to checkpoints, viruses, and prophylaxes, to the dissemination of political power in networked bodies, and to security apparatuses in homes, vehicles, schools, and airports is an important first clue to understanding both the state and subject investments generating wall building today. As already suggested, far from defenses against *international* invasions by other state powers, twenty-first-century walls are responses to *transnational* economic, social, and religious flows that do not have the force of political sovereignty behind them.

81

The new walls target the movements of peoples and goods often drawn by the pull within destination nations for immigrant labor, drugs, weapons, and other contraband, and not only from the press without.[12] Ideologically, the dangers that walls are figured as intercepting are not merely the would-be suicide bomber, but immigrant hordes; not merely violence to the nation, but imagined dilution of national identity through transformed eth-nicized or racial demographics; not merely illegal entrance, but unsustainable pressure on national economies that have ceased to be national or on welfare states that have largely abandoned substantive welfare functions. As such, the new walls defend an inside against an outside where these terms "inside" and "out-side" do not necessarily correspond to nation-state identity or fealty, that is, where otherness and difference are detached from jurisdiction and membership, even as the walls themselves would seem to denote and demarcate precisely these things. Walls today articulate an inside/outside distinction in which what is on the inside and being defended and what is on the outside and being repelled are not particular states or citizens, indeed, in which subjects, political power, political identity, and violence may be territorially detached from states and sovereignty on both sides.

The extent to which inside/outside distinctions comport ever less with the boundaries of nations and the activities of states is evident in the widespread association of new immigrants with danger to the nation, pithily formulated by Valéry Giscard d'Estaing in 1991 — "the problem with which we are now faced has moved from one of immigration to one of invasion" — and more recently by exponents of civilizational clash in Europe, Aus-tralia, and North America.[13] It is apparent, as well, in the grow-ing prevalence and acceptability of two or more legal classes of citizenship in many Western democracies ("regular" citizens, on the one hand, and resident aliens, on the other), something previ-ously associated mainly with nondemocracies, colonial states, or states explicitly striving to preserve a particular religious, ethnic, or racial identity.[14] It is apparent in growing stateless populations

82

composed of refugees from "failed," war-torn, or economically destitute states, refugees whose precise nation of origin becomes lost or irrelevant to their reception elsewhere in the world. It is apparent in the link, whether fantasized or actual, between new immigrant populations inside democracies and threats of terror from without and in illegal drug networks linking supply regions with demand sites. It is apparent in the globally dispersed sources of labor and materials in the manufacture of cars, machinery, electronics, and other consumer goods, a dispersion that makes it increasingly difficult to stamp products and even many firms with a national identity. (Is a Ford a U.S. car or an import?)

In this context, Schmitt's cluster of definitions for the interlocking terms of political life appears to be literally coming apart in late modernity: the sovereign as "he who decides on the exception," the political as turning on the "friend/enemy distinction as the utmost degree of intensity of a union or separation," and the state as the site where sovereignty and the political converge.[15] No longer is the state a consistent embodiment of supreme and decisive power or the agent of a consociation (friends) whose identity is constituted by an identifiable and unified *external* enemy. No longer is the political captured or organizable by state sovereign powers, or, put the other way around, no longer does sovereignty govern or contain the political, by Schmitt's or any other definition. Indeed, from the perspective of the new walls, Schmitt appears as the quintessential owl of Minerva flying at dusk. The concepts he so brilliantly stipulated and braided together in the interwar period were entering the final decades of their modern form.

In addition to responding to globalization's dissolving effects on bounded national economies and demographies, walls respond in terms of both state policies and the anxieties of their subjects to a growing lawlessness lapping the edges of nation-states and streaming across them. This is a lawlessness that is itself a continuous contestation of nation-state sovereignty, abetting its weakening, which is met by exceptional, rather than normal exercises of state power: military, police, and blockading responses, rather than legal and disciplinary practices. Thus, walls do not arise merely because we have "lost control of our borders," a popular truism that Peter Andreas argues "understates the degree to which the state has actually structured, conditioned, and even enabled (often unintentionally) clandestine border crossings, and overstates the degree to which the state has been able to control its borders in the past."[16] The idea of walls as pertaining only to border control also assumes that they pertain to a narrow policing problem of who and what gets in to the nation. It fails to grasp their iconic place in erosions of state sovereignty and coherent nationhood on a more significant scale, erosions that suffuse the psychic, political, economic, and cultural lives of both nations and their subjects and that produce a bundle of conflicting and difficult-to-meet internal and external imperatives for states.

Rather than emanating from the sovereignty of the nation-state, then, the new walls signal the loss of nation-state sovereignty's a priori status and easy link with legal authority, unity, and settled jurisdiction. This condition is evident in the fact that the new walls codify the conflicts to which they respond as permanent and unwinnable. Such codification and militarization of con-tested sovereign authority and law reaches from the land disputes and colonization efforts generating some wall building to the human, drug, and weapon smuggling inciting the construction of others. And while walls might be construed as issuing from or embodying a contingent decisionism that exceeds or supervenes law—*the* sign of sovereignty, according to Schmitt—this is a widely dispersed decisionism that further disseminates state power and hence further weakens the link between the state and sovereignty. Nothing makes this more evident than the vigilan-tism and criminality that accompany walling and that are often integral to the promulgation and course of the new walls.

Settlers in Israel and citizens in the United States and else-where routinely take the law into their own hands to patrol lands, even to apprehend and arrest "illegals," or to make "facts on the ground" in the havoc they sometimes wreak with lands, lives, and livelihoods where the walls are built. Examples abound: There is the Israeli settlers' midnight destruction of Palestinian olive orchards. There is the running skirmish between two opposed activist groups at the U.S.-Mexico border — on one side, the self-anointed "angels" who deposit water and maps in open desert lands north of rural border crossing points, and on the other, the Minutemen who hunt down illegals and collect these materials, sometimes replacing the maps with perfidious ones and the clean water with foul. There is the Israeli Defense Forces' protection of illegal Israeli settlements and settler aggression against their Palestinian neighbors, a practice that led Israeli MP Yuli Tamir to lament: "In a normal country, criminals and security forces are on opposite sides of the fence and do not coordinate their activities."[17] The Israeli case is indeed extreme, but Tamir's lament downplays the extent to which this kind of coordination has become increasingly "normal" at the site of walls where the familiar binaries of law/lawlessness, inside/outside and military/civilian do not hold.

If not sovereign assertions of jurisdiction and law, could the new walls be assimilated to a theoretical frame that casts late modern sovereignty in a permanent "state of exception," where both law and citizenship are suspended? Can they be seen as an element in a new political landscape in which deciding on the juridical exception (posited by Schmitt as the sign of sovereignty) becomes continuous, rather than episodic? In short, might they be assimilated to Giorgio Agamben's thesis that late modern sovereignty has turned in the direction of the "generalization of the state of exception"?[18] Walls, presumably, would signify such a condition insofar as they normalize security conflicts from the center to the edge of sovereign territory and also often remake these edges or broaden or relocate the edge zones, as in the case of the Spanish enclaves in Morocco, the Moroccan appropriation of the Western Sahara, the walling of Kashmir, or the wall winding through the West Bank. In this respect, the new walls would seem to signify a problem usually identified with sovereignty's external face—enmity, rather than order—and run it through the whole of society, producing pockets and islands of walled-in "friends" amid walled-out "enemies." The fantasy of an "us here/them there" rooted in national belonging and state identity cannot be sustained amid the barricaded and checkpointed landscape of postapartheid South Africa, the wall-carved cities of Baghdad and Jerusalem, or the interior checkpoints and gated white communities north of the U.S. border with Mexico. From Agamben's theoretical perspective, walls respond to and extend a condition in which the nation ceases to correspond to the border between friend and enemy and sovereignty instead declares permanent emergency powers to suspend the law and face down enemies everywhere.

If there is insight available from considering walling as an expression of sovereignty in Agamben's terms, there are also limitations to this framing. First, insofar as the network of walls inside, at, across, and beyond nation-states reinforces the detachment of sovereignty from the nation-state, Agamben's argument begs rather than resolves the question of where political sovereignty resides, what or who has it, and whether and why it makes sense to call hyperbolic and extralegal expressions of state power "sovereign." Second, an argument that would cast the new walls as exercises of sovereign political power, rather than as failures of it, occludes the extent to which a so-called "permanent state of exception" represents a state of emergency for state sovereignty itself, and not only for the nation. That is, exceptionality cannot become permanent without eroding the norm defining it and against which it functions, without replacing that norm with itself and thereby forfeiting the status of exceptionality through which sovereignty is defined. Third, this framing would eschew an important aspect of walling, namely, its imbrication with sovereign practices disseminated to citizens, the military, and the police, that is, with a local "decisionism" exercised by each that further undermines unified and consolidated state sovereignty.

These last two points require elaboration. If walls are in part weapons against a permanent disorder and illegality both at the boundaries of nation-states and coursing through them, if they are among the new technologies of power responding to the limitations or even breakdown of the rule of law *and* order in sovereign nations, they are in this regard continuous with the extrajuridical practices springing up everywhere—those concerning "enemy noncombatants" and facilitating torture and political assassinations, those structuring the Guantánamo gulag and "renditions" of captured prisoners, those setting aside domestic laws to build the U.S.-Mexico wall, and those permitting the building of the Israeli wall in Palestinian territory despite verdicts against its current route delivered by both the International Court of Justice and the Israeli Supreme Court. This would seem to comport with Agamben's argument about the sovereign suspension of law and citizenship in a permanent state of emergency. However, in the case of walling, this extrajuridicism is not limited to state or sovereign prerogative, but rather occurs largely through the blurring of military, police, and citizen prerogatives at the site of walls, a blurring that challenges the state monopoly on decisionism as well as the monopoly on violence presumed to anchor state sovereignty.[19]

A striking instance of this blurring appears in the recent construction of a portion of border fencing in Naco, Arizona, undertaken by the Minutemen, a well-known and well-organized vigilante group. On private property in this small town seventy-five miles east of the secured port of entry at Nogales, the Minutemen funded, designed, and built a mile-long barrier made of thirteen-foot-high heavy-gauge welding mesh that can neither be climbed nor cut with conventional tools. This endeavor appeared aimed in part at showing an inept and inefficient Department of Homeland Security how to do its work, and in this regard expresses a certain antistatism, or at least disdain toward the bureaucratic and legal weightedness of liberal democratic states. On the Web site describing the volunteer construction work, the Minutemen first decry the lack of state action on the "security crisis plaguing our nation" and then declare that "SOMEONE needs to do something—and now, someone IS: The Minuteman Civil Defense

Corps is building a REAL border fence along the U.S.-Mexico border!"[20] Of course, the Minutemen are aiming to shore up, rather than to deplete state power—indeed, to incite that power to shore up itself, to "force our feckless federal government to recognize the need to protect American citizens and territory." Implying that the Minutemen have an intact masculinity that the state may have lost and needs to recoup, the text continues: "The Minuteman Border Fence was created to put steel in the ground and demonstrate the feasibility and affordability of securing the border" in order to protect "America's sovereign territory against incursion, invasion, and terrorism."[21] Moreover, as the Minutemen struggle to prop up faltering state sovereignty, the state has become a willing partner with this outlaw group: Significantly, atop the fence they built, the Minutemen mounted video cameras that stream directly to the Nogales dispatch offices of the U.S. Border Patrol. In this fusion of state and parastate powers and in this appropriation of state prerogative which is then relayed back to the state, political sovereignty suffers a further deterioration. Indeed, it weakens at the very site of its incitation by vigilantes.

An event along the Texas portion of the border provides an instance of dissemination of state sovereignty initiated from the opposite direction. Early in 2007, the governor of Texas authorized a $5 million project to install video cameras on sections of the federally funded Texas-Mexico border fence. These cameras stream to an open Internet site so that "web users worldwide can watch the border and phone the authorities if they spot apparently illegal crossings."[22] As the state outsources security in this way, its own status as sovereign protector declines. There is an additional paradox of insecurity produced by this kind of outsourcing: No one can make better use of such border-watching technology than vigilantes and those in the increasingly sophisticated illegal border-crossing industry that the technology aims to thwart.[23]

In addition to the vigilante activity supplementing and hence undercutting state authority at the actual site of walls, there are telling emergences on the Internet that embody this blurring.

Consider "usborderpatrol.com," whose name, logo, and Web design make it appear, at first blush, as the official Web site of the U.S. Border Patrol.[24] In fact, the site is maintained by anonymous "supporters of the United States Border Patrol" evidently frustrated by the agency's insufficient attention to public relations, political mobilization, and education, and frustrated, as well, by laconic Homeland Security policies and technologies related to border security. Nor is the personification of sovereign authority limited to Web site graphics or design. A page entitled "A Border Patrol Moment" (taken down from the site since this chapter was written), featured a dramatic account of the duties, capacities, and ordinary practices of the Border Patrol in a voice resonant of rogue police bravado and authority. The reader, interpellated as an outsider or smuggler seeking to drive into the U.S. at an official port of entry, was addressed in a snide, intimidating, and even menacing style—the sort peculiar to power that has contempt for its subjects, enjoys toying with them a bit, and is not being monitored for its professionalism or conduct—in short, the sort one can well imagine at the gateway between the First and Third Worlds. Miranda rights were also casually ridiculed, and the "immense powers...rarely exercised" of the U.S. agents were underlined.[25] Interestingly, however, while the Web-site text was evidently addressed to an alien "you" seeking to gain illegal entry into the United States, it was written entirely in English. Thus, it would not appear to be warning or educating this "you," but rather performing the power of the Border Patrol for United States citizens who might be dubious about the validity or effectiveness of that power and in a fashion that the Border Patrol itself cannot publicly employ. In this way, usborderpatrol.com undertakes a curious kind of public relations for the Border Patrol, one that attempts to prop up its power in part by underscoring the liberties the Border Patrol can take with the law and with its subjects, a distinctly sovereign function that is also being impersonated by the vigilante group itself. Here again is an instance of a new form of political decisionism or extralegality emerging

in the wake of nation-state sovereignty, a practice of vigilan-
tism that, through its very act of propping up state sovereignty,
inadvertently undoes its aim to supplement the state's faltering
power to defend the nation. These efforts at border fortification
disseminate and hence undo precisely the state sovereignty they
would resurrect.

As already suggested, this undoing of sovereignty is expressed
as well in the ways the walls codify the challenges to which
they respond as permanent and unwinnable. This is expressed,
too, in the fact that many of the new walls do not merely border, but invent the societies they limn. Such walls may be bids
to augment existing sovereignties, or to bring into being new
nonstate political consociations, or to reinvigorate old dividing
lines: "sort-of-greater Israel," Fortress Europe, Southern Africa,
a greater Morocco, or North America versus South America.
Importantly, while these alliances and divisions may correspond
to certain state interests, they cannot be precisely identified with
settled sovereigns or nation-states as such. Nor is the disjuncture
between walls and sovereign jurisdiction limited to projects of
current or future annexation, such as the penetration of Israel's
wall deep into Palestinian territory or the Moroccan wall cutting
through the Western Sahara. The Israeli wall marks neither two
states nor one and is not a self-consistent bid for either, just as the
walls of apartheid and postapartheid South Africa or the "peace
lines" striating Belfast and Derry aim neither to divide nor to
unite those entities. Rather, as monuments to unsettled and unse-
cured sovereignty, these walls institutionalize a condition whose
opposite their designers would have them performatively enact.

Theatricalizing Sovereignty

An Arizona rancher and former Marine declared to a journalist:
"They built this wall as a showpiece, so Americans can see it and
say, 'Oh, yeah, that'll stop 'em.' It might stop a large, TV-watch-
ing gringo. But somebody coming from Oaxaca who's hungry
and wants a job, it isn't going to stop him. It's a Band-Aid on a

sucking chest wound. The whole thing is phony."[26] While the new walls sometimes effectively interdict the foreign bodies deemed dangerous to what they limn, they are often nothing more than spectacularly expensive political gestures, sops to certain constituencies, signs of what distresses but cannot be contained, as irrelevant to the project of national security as the scrupulous wanding and suitcase disemboweling of a random traveler through the Des Moines airport.

Consider: Operation Gatekeeper produced, at the San Diego/ Tijuana border, three layers of fifteen-foot-high steel walls, adorned with sensors and video surveillance technology and monitored by hundreds of Border Patrol officers in jeeps and helicopters. For ten years following its construction, just thirty miles to the east, the border was marked by a dilapidated and easily scalable fence constructed of Vietnam-era air force landing mats. Even now, the meager vehicle and pedestrian border barriers outside the city contrast starkly with those inside. This story is repeated at the other urban border crossing points in Arizona, New Mexico, and Texas.[27]

For would-be migrants, whether temporary or permanent, the effect of the spectacular new fortifications is to require a longer, more expensive, and harrowing journey—through mountains and deserts—than before the walls were built. (In the past thirteen years, there have been at least five thousand migrant deaths along the U.S.-Mexico border.) This effect produces a chain of others: among them, an exponential increase in the sophistication, size, and profit of smuggling operations and a greater likelihood that illegal entrants will stay and settle in the United States, rather than enter for seasonal work and then return home.

Border expert Peter Andreas argues forthrightly that the new walls have "less to do with actual deterrence [than] with managing the image of the border." He adds: "Border policing is a ritualistic performance. When the failures of the deterrence effort lead to a performance crisis, the performers save face by promising a bigger and better show.... And in the case of immigration control, the crackdown on illegal crossings along the most visible stretches of the border has erased politically embarrassing images of chaos and replaced them with comforting images of order."[28]

Mike Davis is, characteristically, even more blunt:

> San Diego's triple wall and similar medieval fortifications in Arizona and Texas are political stage sets. Operation Gatekeeper (the San Diego wall), for instance, was undertaken by the Clinton administration at the instigation of Democratic senator Dianne Feinstein in order to wrest the border issue away from California Republicans. The militarization of the border was designed to send the message that the Democrats were not "soft" on illegal immigration. Feinstein indeed has made frequent use of the new steel wall as a backdrop for press conferences. The tripling of the wall under the G. W. Bush administration, meanwhile, was an up-the-ante move by conservative San Diego congressman Duncan Hunter [chair of the House Armed Services Committee] to show he was even tougher on the border than Feinstein.[29]

Walls provide spectacular backdrops for politicians and parties facing quagmired immigration and amnesty policies and who are concerned to cultivate racialized constituencies on both sides of the immigration divide. They also resurrect an image of the state as sustaining the very powers of protection and self-determination challenged by terrorist technologies, on one side, and neoliberal capitalism, on the other. They are potential spectacles of such protection and self-determination and more generally of the resolve and capacity for action identified with the political autonomy generated by sovereignty. If this figuration is an illusion, that does not cancel its importance in offering what Andreas calls "an appealing political salve for an extraordinarily difficult set of problems that have no easy short-term solutions."[30] In some cases, their political effect even depends upon their functional irrelevance. As one cynical rancher at the Arizona-Mexico border put it, with the new wall, "the government isn't controlling the border, it's controlling what Americans *think* about the border."[31]

Economist Jagdish Bhagwati makes a similar point when describing India's first effort at walling out Bangladesh: "While late Prime Minister Indira Gandhi's decision to construct a fence along the enormous India-Bangladesh border ... was an ineffective policy ... it was nevertheless a splendid policy. For, to be seen to be doing nothing at all, even though one could not really close the border, would have been politically explosive.... And building the fence was the least disruptive way of doing nothing while appearing to be doing something."[32]

Joseph Nevins brings into view still another dimension of the contribution of walls to the theatrics of propping up sovereignty. Operation Gatekeeper, Nevins argues, "has largely failed to protect the national citizenry from the 'threat' presented by 'illegals.'" But with the wall, the "U.S.-Mexico boundary in high-visibility or highly urbanized areas appear far more *orderly* than it did several years ago."[33] This appearance, in turn, restores a more general "sense of order" in and for the nation. Order, it will be recalled, is an important leitmotif in Schmitt's account of the provisions of political sovereignty. In one of his characteristic inversions, Schmitt argues that it is sovereignty, rather than law, that provides order. This is evidenced both by sovereignty's capacity to suspend the law in the name of order and by the fact that "the legal order itself rests on a decision not a norm."[34] Sovereignty acting in the "exception," Schmitt argues, dissolves "the two elements of the concept legal order ... into independent notions ... and thereby testif[ies] to their conceptual independence."[35] Thus does a wall's production of an apparently more orderly border stage a sovereign capacity and effect woefully limited by globalization — that of producing political order as such.

Importantly, the performances described by Andreas, Bhagwati, Davis, and Nevins do not simply respond to existing nationalism or racism. Rather, they activate and mobilize them in the face of a nest of economic and political problems issuing contradictory imperatives with regard to borders in a globalized era. The staging of sovereign integrity, order, and force in the face of sovereign decline both draws upon and intensifies a xenophobic sense of nationhood among the nation's subjects. To see more clearly how this performance operates, we need to turn to the economy-security nexus within which walls are staged and to which they contribute.

The stated objectives of the Smart Borders Action Plan (SBAP) formulated by the United States Department of Homeland Security and signed by Canada and the United States in December 2001 offer an exemplary rhetorical account of the economic and security imperatives constructing contemporary border fortifications. These objectives are "to develop a zone of confidence against terrorist activity" and to "create a unique opportunity to build a smart border for the 21st century, a border that allows the secure, free flow of people and goods, a border that reflects the largest trading relationship in the world."[36] This mix of biopower taken to the international level (achieving "the secure, free flow of people and goods"), theatricality practiced in the name of governance (creating "a zone of confidence against terrorist activity") and updated classic Realpolitik (building "a smart border for the 21st century") emblematizes the complex national, postnational, and transnational economy and security contexts of the new walls.

The conventional wisdom about neoliberal globalization is that it produces opposing economy and security imperatives, with the former driving toward the elimination of barriers and the latter toward border fortification. Thus, an economically driven erasure of distinctions between peoples, cultures, states, or currencies is countered by a security-motivated press for boundaries and closure. Geographer Mathew Coleman argues that this tension erodes state sovereignty as it disunifies it: "A constitutive tension between a rebordering national security territoriality and a debordering geography of participation in open markets and trade networks" means that "geopolitical and geoeconomic practice, rather than the coherent product of a properly sovereign center of policy power capable of balancing and managing diverse security and trade agendas, is a field or network of policy designs whose exercise over space is far from orderly."[37] Because border policy formulated under these conditions can be decentered to the point of incoherence, Coleman warns left critics, in particular, against casting such policy as emerging from the consolidated interests of states or capital.

However, the notion of a tension between security and economy imperatives does not adequately capture the security-economy nexus out of which the new walls emerge. Close consideration of both sets of imperatives undoes the simple formulation in which economic interests drive toward unbordering and security interests toward rebordering.

What the conventional narrative articulates as security issues are often in fact consequences of neoliberal globalization, and contrary to the received wisdom, economic imperatives frequently produce what are characterized as security concerns. As such, they lead to walls and walling, not to open borders and the free flow of labor, capital, goods, and services. While many of its proponents frame neoliberalism as an *alternative* to the wars, coups, struggle, and strife of Realpolitik and paint a picture of a global order pacified by economic integration, it is no secret that neoliberal reforms are often ushered in by or generate a palpable share of violence that results in new security concerns for every region they touch. Violence induced or exploited to impose free-market reforms, dubbed "disaster capitalism" by Naomi Klein, characterized events and policies in Chile and Argentina in the 1970s, China in the late 1980s, Russia in the 1990s, Iraq after the U.S. invasion, even New Orleans in the wake of Hurricane Katrina.[38] In addition to paving the way for the neoliberalization of certain regimes and regions, violence is also a crucial part of the effects of neoliberalism. These effects appear in the devastation of regions dependent for generations on industries that suddenly collapse or relocate; in the making of global slums where gang-controlled underground economies prevail; in the spawning of such desperate poverty in the Global South that inhabitants risk lives and the permanent loss of families to become woefully paid and socially disparaged illegal day laborers in the North; in the transmogrification of rice farmers in rural Thailand to lottery-ticket sellers and prostitutes on the streets of Bangkok; or in the stream of Bangladeshis trudging to Calcutta for better prospects.

Neoliberalism's lightning-fast relocations of the scenes of production, rapidly rising and falling currencies and prices, and other vicissitudes of economic life thus produce what Hannah Arendt analyzed fifty years ago as masses of (stateless) peoples reduced to "bare life," people so politically disqualified and untethered, hence so little anointed by political markers of humanness, that the new walls appear as a kind of cage against their animal-like "invasion."[39] (*The Third World Invasion* is the title of Pat Buchanan's screed against lax U.S. immigration enforcement and "invading immigrant hordes" is a standard figure in arguments for closed borders.) Indeed, if there remains any validity to the humanist and especially democratic conceit about speech, recognition, law, and freedom as markers of the distinctively human, these mute barricades deny these capacities both to the beings they would repel and in the power they represent, thus tacitly snubbing the universal humanism promulgated by the putatively global moral discourse of democracy and of human rights and tacitly degrading democracy at the same time.

The effects of neoliberalism on security issues are also mirrored in populations whose lawlessness pertains not merely to their visa status, but to participation in the traffic in drugs, sex, weapons, terrorism, or petty criminality that many of the new walls would aim to interdict. Foucault reminds us that neoliberal rationality, which exceeds the economic sphere and permeates the political and the social with market values, has a corrosive effect on the rule of law as this rationality molds both individual and state activity to entrepreneurial criteria.[40] These criteria displace the supremacy of law and every other supervenient moral authority. This displacement occurs both at the level of neoliberal statism, a process dubbed by Foucault the "governmentalization"

of the state, which involves the remaking of the state on the model of the firm, and at the level of individuals, their remaking from complex moral subjects into "specks of human capital" who self-invest to appreciate their value.[41] In short, neoliberal states and subjects alike are interpellated and configured by measures of profitability, capital appreciation, and effectivity, measures that supplant law and other principles normatively binding conduct.[42] Moreover, as neoliberal political rationality erases the strong distinction between criminal and legal entrepreneurial activity, it also legitimates the production of an ever-growing underclass that is "in, but not of" the global order. "The criminal," Thomas Lemke writes in his description of Foucault's study of neoliberalism "is a rational economic individual who invests, expects a certain profit and risks making a loss.... For the neoliberals, crime is no longer located outside the market model, but is instead one market among others."[43] In short, given neoliberalism's imbrication with political violence, demographic upheavals and deracinations and its corrosive effects on law's moral standing, it is difficult, if not impossible to separate the dimensions of security and economy that structure international border politics.

Even if they could be distinguished, walls cannot be placed easily on the security side of a "security versus economy" matrix of contrary pulls toward bordering and unbordering. Such matrices continue to presume sovereign nation-states and the autonomy of the political and the economic. They also lack a place for the symbolic and theatrical dimensions of border fortifications. At best, staying strictly within an economy-security framing, walls could be characterized as (feeble) technologies in the "war of all" generated by neoliberalism itself, security measures responding to economically generated forces that themselves break down the legal spaces conventionally organized by political sovereignty and represented by nation-states. Walls represent the emergence of policing and barricading in the face of this breakdown and of the ungovernability by law and politics of forces produced by globalization and, in some cases, late modern colonialization.

97

Walls also emerge as part of the ad hoc regulatory and protectionist apparatuses of neoliberalism, apparatuses sometimes difficult to see amid neoliberalism's formal disavowal of both regulation and protectionism. Some critics have gone so far as to argue that the new walls constitute the ideal regulatory scheme for neoliberalism, regulating flows of labor and goods while permitting the unrestricted flow of capital.[44] However, like the claim that security and economy imperatives generate opposing bordering and unbordering tendencies, this neo-Marxist account oversimplifies neoliberal imperatives and also neglects the theatrical and theological dimensions of walls.

Like earlier forms of capitalist governance, neoliberal governance is complicated by tensions between capital and labor and between various sectors within each about desirable levels and objects of national protectionism. Labor, organized and unorganized, wants to keep its own value high by restricting flows of cheap foreign labor, yet on the consumption front, it wants access to cheap foreign goods. Capital, large and small, seeks unrestricted flows of cheap labor and would restrict flows of competing products. Thus, walls cannot simply be regarded as tools of capital with indifference to what they perform symbolically and materially. As we have already seen, even the most physically ominous new walls do not bar flows of illegal immigrant labor, and economic cycles of boom and bust affect both the size of those flows and state responses to them. Davis reports dramatic variations in numbers of undocumented immigrants and enforcement actions against U.S. employers according to the expansion and contraction of the economy: "During the recession of the early 1990s...the U.S. Immigration and Naturalization Service conducted massive raids on Latino worksites. Some 14,000 enforcement actions were taken against employers of illegal immigrants during 1991. In the booming economy of the late 1990s, however, the INS downgraded workplace immigration enforcement in order to accommodate a soaring demand for minimum-wage labor. It issued a mere 150 sanctions in 2001."[45]

These vacillations in enforcement efforts and immigration rates are not lost on border communities. One Texan residing near the wall remarks: "I think politicians and corporate America are in cahoots to override our immigration laws...they're making big money off this cheap labor.... This wall is a way to make it look like they're doing something."[46] Similarly, only in the most recent phase of the occupation has Israel reduced long-standing reliance on hundreds of thousands of legal and illegal Palestinian day laborers, a phenomenon both economies depended on and both polities decried.[47] When this reliance finally produced too great a political cost, Israel solved its need for cheap labor first with temporarily imported Southeast Asian and Eastern European workers and then with Jewish immigrants from the former Soviet Union and Ethiopa.[48]

One commentator sums up walls' contribution to economic regulation this way: "Porous walls that produce not closure but hundreds...of entries and crossings" mirror the "temporary legality" of the *bracero* program and other guest-worker policies, both formal and informal.[49] Walls embody and facilitate the liminality between law and nonlaw important to flexible production, but not because they are straightforward instruments of capital or because they are efficacious in their aims. That argument occludes capital's oscillating and contradictory needs, occludes other incitements to walling and the performative effects of walling, and implies a systematic political capacity that capital rarely harbors. Rather, it is the intersection of law and exception at the site of walls that generates a body of labor outside the law, labor that is neither organized nor protected, and that increases the number of usable and disposable subjects who are not citizens. This effect is certainly one that capital can exploit but it is not one it can produce on its own.

What about the other half of the conventional wisdom about contemporary bordering and unbordering? If no systematic argument can be made that contemporary economic imperatives drive toward open borders and unrestricted flows of labor and goods across them, do security imperatives press toward fortifications and closure—toward walling? This, too, is dubious. Security today requires not just containment, but movement, flow, openness, and availability to inspection. Nothing is more dangerous than potential sedition or insurgency hidden in closed cells, on the one hand, or a stubbornly immoveable, untransformable, inassimilable, or otherwise fixed and insulated minority population, on the other. Security requires not only the ability to survey, inspect, process, count, and record, but the ability to channel, transfer, relocate, or simply drive out certain populations. The checkpoint rather than the barrier, the Plexiglas booth rather than the windowless cell, video surveillance rather than the guarded door, the tripped alarm rather than the iron gate—these are the contemporary signatures of securitization. Indeed, a security dilemma often identified in regard to the Israeli barrier is that the solid, high wall that blocks bullets and other explosives also blocks clear surveillance and the access needed for subduing armed challenges. "It is easier to shoot through a fence than it is through a wall"—the truism applies equally to the border guard and her armed target.[50] Barricades thus generate new security dilemmas as they aim to solve existing ones.

Security and economy issues also intertwine in walls' generation of unintended effects. Sometimes these are as prosaic as "security" walls slicing through the farmland or cutting off supply access roads of those living at the border.[51] But sometimes they are more dramatic: Fifteen years of U.S.-Mexico border fortification have spawned a hugely profitable and efficient migrant- and drug-smuggling industry, one that does not remain confined to border zones, but generates escalating levels of violence from drug gangs deep inside both nations. Or consider the impact of the Israeli "security fence" on what remains of the Palestinian economy—enormous downward pressure on GNP, choked supplies of producer and consumer goods and services, deteriorating infrastructure, high rates of unemployment. While this may serve certain Israeli state interests in producing an ever-weaker and less appealing Palestine, it also broadens and intensifies Palestinian resistance to Israeli domination.

Finally, economy and security issues interpenetrate as legitimating discourses in the production and promotion of walls. To begin with, the dissemination of neoliberal rationality, which overtakes liberal democratic political values and institutions with its single calculus of profitability and efficiency, itself facilitates the legitimacy of walling and encampment across putatively democratic societies. When commitments to universal equality and liberty cede the field to cost-benefit accounting in political and legal life, not only does "walled democracy" cease to offend the (vanishing) core values of the society that it claims to protect, the "hypocrisy" of walls that themselves often organize illegality is barely registered as such. Add to this post-9/11 discourses allowing security to trump liberal democratic principles and commitments, and the walls' fusion of permanent policing and militarization, racial profiling, and extralegality all become assimilable, if not affirmed, in societies calling themselves democracies.

Security, economy, and geopolitical imperatives are also often mobilized to dissimulate one another in the promotion and development of walling. Israel's wall and before it, Israeli settlements in the 1970s, were built in the name of "security" even as they constituted a land-grab amid insecure and uncertain sovereignties.[52] In the post-9/11 period, the U.S.-Mexico wall has been promulgated by politicians and citizen groups alike on national-security grounds. "Terrorists love open borders: Remember 9/11," one group sloganizes on behalf of the U.S.-Mexico wall.[53] Or, as a Weneedafence.com Web page declares: "In addition to the hundreds of thousands of illegal immigrants from Central and South America, there are several hundreds, perhaps thousands ... of illegal aliens from countries that sponsor terrorism or harbor terrorists entering the United States each year across our border with Mexico. ... Similar fences [in Israel] have reduced terrorist attacks by up to 95%."[54]

Weneedafence.com exemplifies the mobilization of security concerns—fear—on behalf of economic ones. But what one also sees in this merger, and particularly in the identification of the United States with Israel as a target for terrorism, are the operations of racism and xenophobia in this mobilization, operations the walls themselves meld as they barricade the nation against what they produce as a dark, dangerous, and threatening outside. Consider, in this regard, the following poem prominently placed since 2006 on the Weneedafence.com Web site.

An Open Border
by Scott Rohter

Take some bricks and build a wall
Make it solid, strong and tall.
Let it stretch from gulf to sea
That safer at home we all may be.
Build it wide from rim to rim
So terrorists and smugglers can't sneak in;
And make it deep, secure from holes
Through which flow the drugs that wreck our souls.
Stop the drug trade in its tracks.
Keep us safe from terrorist attacks.
And let it stand the test of time
I pray, keep safe this land of mine.

Consider this, that it's your job
To keep those out who would rape and rob;
From this great cause you cannot run
While so many of us have lost daughter and son.
You ask our children to serve and fight;
They trust their leaders to do what's right.
And what's right is this—it's easy to see;
It's plain and simple, as one, two three—
If you'll keep us safe in the war on terror
An open border is a fatal error.[55]

It is easy to deride or dismiss as reactionary ignorance Rohter's metonymic chains of terrorism, smuggling, drugs, rape and robbery, and illegal immigrants, on one side, and solidity, strength, height, Christian prayer, service, safety, and children righteously sacrificed in wars of freedom, on the other. Such metonymies, however, both reveal the anxieties generated by declining state sovereignty and discursively resurrect myths of viable state sovereignty and of a homogenous and autarkic nation-state contained and protected by such sovereignty. The arch oppositions between these two metonymic chains both stage a division between the (good) interior and (evil) exterior of the nation and distract from the fusions and confusions at the site of walls between inside and outside, military and police, civilians and soldiers, immigrants and terrorists, lawless vigilantes and aspiring entrants seeking reprieve from economic destitution.[56] They distract, too, from the paradoxes of walled democracy and of nations settled by immigrants—the United States, Israel, Canada, Australia—now targeting immigrants as the enemy. (Compare Rohter's poem with the inscription at an older port of U.S. entry: "Give me your tired, your poor, your huddled masses yearning to breathe free, the wretched refuse of your teeming shore.") Like the old Bantustans separating white South Africans physically and ontologically from the African labor on which their existence depended, the new walls contribute to organizing this dependency, even as they visually articulate autarky, separation, and antagonism. The new walls thus dissimulate need and dependency as they resurrect myths of national autonomy and purity in a globalized world. Danger, disorder, and violence are projected outside, and sovereign power is figured as securing a homogeneous, orderly, and safe national interior.

The Theological Remainder: Sovereign Awe
The new walls have been compared to dams insofar as they are built to regulate, rather than impede flows.[57] But they are like dams in another respect: They are often visual signifiers of

overwhelming human power and state capacity, and in the context of receding sovereignty, they project a restored sovereign power to decide, delimit, protect, and repel. They visually encase the nation as a protected compound and present to the outside world a mighty national shield. It is the effect of this spectacle of power that helps explain not just the current contagion of border fortification among nations, but the move to build mammoth and imposing walls, rather than (potentially) more effective and less expensive virtual barriers using sensors and alarms. In the context of sovereign decline, walls stage a dimension of sovereignty described by Hobbes as overawing and which is likened by Hobbes to God's power. According to Hobbes, both divine and political sovereignty rule and bind by overawing all. Sovereignty is not merely a superior or supreme power, but one that collectively subdues its individual subjects with its majesty and might.[58] Chapter 2 began with the argument that the enclosure brings the sacred into being. A mammoth wall recalls the awe-inducing effects of the divine and of sovereignty's basis in it. In a time of waning nation-state sovereignty, it is the material embodiment of this theological remainder.

Walls also contribute to the imaginary of intact nationhood to which such a sovereignty would correspond. Walls, "solid, strong, and tall," redress faltering distinctions between us and them, inside and outside, law and nonlaw, with a singularly striking visual icon of these distinctions. Walls are unrivaled means of signifying a divide between us and them, between our space and theirs, between inside and outside, the domestic and the exterior. Thus, at the same time that walls dissimulate declining state sovereignty with a spectacle of its rectitude and might, walls cleave the reality of global interdependence and global disorder with stage set productions of intact nationhood, autonomy and self-sufficiency. They resurrect the imagined space and people of the nation that sovereignty would contain and protect.

As scenes of awe, rather than efficacy, and of force rather than right, the new walls stage sovereign power in its most theological dross. We are thus reminded again that waning state sovereignty often reveals sovereignty's theological aspect more directly even as it decants the two powers it was originally established to contain, religion as well as political economy. We are reminded, too, of the contemporary susceptibility of politics and its subjects to theological motifs, a susceptibility evident in the popular desire for walls, a susceptibility generated by their effects and inscribed on the walls themselves as sovereignty's theological face. It is not incidental that Rohter's poem is framed as a prayer and addressed to the state.[59]

CHAPTER FOUR

Desiring Walls

The spectacle is the material reconstruction of the religious illusion.
—Guy Debord, *Society of the Spectacle*

Israel is a villa in the jungle.
—Ehud Barak

I think the fence is least effective. But I'll build the goddamned fence if they want it.
—Senator John McCain

You show me a 50-foot fence and I'll show you a 51-foot ladder at the border.
—U.S. Department of Homeland Security Secretary Janet Napolitano

Why do late modern subjects desire nation-state walls, and what do walls promise to secure, protect, rehabilitate, contain, or keep at bay? To what extent does the spectacle of a wall gratify a wish for sovereignty restored to the subject, as well as to the state? This chapter considers the effects of waning state sovereignty on the psychic-political desires, anxieties, and needs of late modern subjects. It theorizes the contemporary frenzy of nation-state wall building, especially in Western democracies, from the vantage point of a subject made vulnerable by the loss of horizons, order, and identity attending the decline of state sovereignty. It asks what psychic reassurances or palliatives walls provide amid these losses. It asks as well what fantasies of innocence, protection, homogeneity, and self-sufficiency walls secure.

These queries in turn open two avenues of analytic possibility. On the one hand, the subject may *identify* with the attenuated potency of the state occasioned by declining sovereignty and seek measures that restore this potency. Here, the nation-state's vulnerability and unboundedness, permeability and violation, are felt as the subject's own. Such identification, with its gendered and sexual connotations, would seem to be at the heart of the aggrieved masculinism of the Minutemen's walling campaign. (Recall from Chapter 3 the Minutemen's desire to "put steel into the ground" to recover control of sovereign territory and indeed, sovereignty itself.) Such identification between the subject and the state is no doubt an element of all forms of militarized nationalism.

On the other hand, the effect of eroding political sovereignty on the power of the state to provide protection and security for its subjects may threaten the sovereignty of subjects more directly. The specter of transnational terrorism, for example, translates state vulnerability directly into the vulnerability of subjects. But terrorism does not exhaust the matter. Recall the circuitry, identified in Chapter 2, that the social contract establishes between political and individual sovereignty. This circuitry both premises the contract (individuals are sovereign in the state of nature, but insecurely so) and is also transformed by the contract (sovereign individuality is what the social contract promises to establish and secure). From Hobbes to Locke, Rousseau to Rawls, political sovereignty is generated by the prepolitical sovereignty of the subject in the state of nature and legitimated by the postcontractual sovereignty of the subject in society. The sovereign state brings into being and secures the sovereign social subject, even as it appropriates that subject's political sovereignty for the making of its own.

These two different dimensions of the state-subject relation, identification and production, are both important in generating the desire for walls in late modern liberal societies, where the social contract remains ideologically and discursively constitutive. Undoubtedly these two dimensions of the state-subject relation are pertinent to nonliberal societies, as well, and hence to walling in such societies. However, these relations would necessarily have different contours and contents from those produced by liberal social contractarianism, a difference left unexplored in this chapter.

One additional prefatory note is in order: This chapter argues that nation-state walling responds in part to psychic fantasies, anxieties, and wishes and does so by generating visual effects and a national imaginary apart from what walls purport to "do." Walls may be effective in producing this psychic containment even as they fail to block or repel the transnational and clandestine flows of people, goods, and terror both that signal and contribute to the undermining of political sovereignty. Walling responds in this regard to subject desires that are themselves the effect of declining sovereignty, desires that states can neither gratify nor ignore. The fact that walls do not and cannot actually stop or even effectively mitigate these transnational flows is an important part of this argument. Thus, prior to examining the desire for walls, we first need to return to the failure of walls to achieve their putative aims.

The Inefficacy of Walls

Walls have many substantive effects on the political identity and subjectivity of those they separate, on the lives and lands of those in or near their path, and on the prospects for integration or peace settlements in conflicts that they consecrate. However, walls do little to halt the illegal migration, drug smuggling, or terrorism most frequently and overtly animating and legitimating them, and the reason for this is simple: immigrants, smugglers, and terrorists are not entering nations because land borders are lax and are thus not deterred by border fortifications, though their activities may be rerouted and otherwise transformed by them. Walls may augment the technologies, cost, social organization, experiences, and meaning of what they purport to lock out, but they are relatively ineffective as interdiction. As one U.S. Immigration and Customs Enforcement agent summed up the matter, "It's like squeezing a balloon. The air has got to go somewhere."[1]

But don't some walls attain their publicly declared aims? Hasn't Israel built such a wall? True, the Israeli wall, in combination with multiplied and fortified checkpoints and a complex network of roads, bridges, tunnels, and train systems aimed at surgically separating Palestinians from Israelis in an intricately intimate geography, may have reduced suicide bombing in Tel Aviv...although many argue that Hamas was committing itself to alternative paramilitary strategy and tactics even as the Wall was being conceived. What is certain is that the Wall has not reduced Palestinian violence and hostility toward Israel, improved prospects of a political settlement, or generated greater international sympathy and hence political capital for Israel. Clearly, the Wall *has* produced new political subjectivities on both sides and is part of a larger architecture of occupation separating Palestinians from Israelis and discursively inverting the sources and circuitries of violence, projecting the cause of the wall onto imagined originary Palestinian aggression toward Israel.[2] One could say that these effects of the Wall, along with its redrawing of the Israel-Palestine map to include a number of West Bank Israeli settlements within Israeli territory, are all part of the policy aims of walling. But precisely insofar as the Wall is legitimated, indeed, often lamented, entirely on the grounds of making Israel secure from Palestinian hostilities, its inefficacy in this regard is striking. Building a wall has not stopped Palestinian violence or hostility, only altered Palestinian tactics and technologies, even as it has exacerbated frustration and rage at Israeli domination.

Israel is the hard case for my argument. Much easier are the walls formally aimed at interdicting migrant labor, illegal drugs, and other contraband. As the previous chapter suggested, by most scholarly accounts, the U.S.-Mexico wall, which has now been authorized, though not fully funded, to be built across the entire two-thousand-mile border, is a political theater piece, albeit an exceptionally expensive one in a number of respects. Labor from south of the border has been vital to the North American economy since the building of the railroads in the West two centuries ago. In the last two decades, globalization has dramatically increased both the quantity of this migration and the value of keeping it illegal.[3] Northern capital today requires labor that is maximally cheap and exploitable—hirable at subminimum wage, without benefits or regard for regulations on overtime, health, environment, or safety, and easily dispatched when not needed. In the face of growing global competition, such labor has become increasingly important to the construction and manufacturing industries and to the retail and fast-food sectors, not only to the domestic and agricultural work with which it has long been associated.

The building of a wall pretending to halt the immigration of labor required by capital produces an abundance of ironies. There is the story of the Golden State Fence Company, a firm that built a significant portion of the border wall in Southern California, which was charged three times over a decade with having hundreds of undocumented workers on its payroll.[4] There are the repeated immigration raids on McDonald's franchises across the United States for hiring undocumented workers to flip its all-American burgers. These ironies have their cousins in Israel, not only in the form of Palestinians employed to build the Wall, but in the remarkable story of a protest against the proposed route of the Wall by women of an illegal Israeli settlement because the route blocked access to their homes by maids from a neighboring Palestinian village.[5]

The story is similar with drugs: As Europeans recognize to a greater degree than North Americans, drug smuggling does not drive drug use. Rather, the demand for drugs pulls the supply. Several studies, including one by the RAND Corporation, have shown that to reduce drug demand in the North, substance-abuse treatment yields far more bang for the buck than border reinforcements, the main effect of which is to increase drug prices.[6] But what sells politically are walls and elaborate sting operations, not drug-rehabilitation facilities, let alone policies that address the social conditions generating drug markets in North America.

More than simply failing, however, walls often compound the problems they putatively address. First, because walling and other border-intensification measures make migration more difficult and expensive, they tend to increase one-directional migration, thus enlarging the numbers of illegal migrants living permanently in the United States or Europe. Second, walls armed at drugs and immigration produce an ever more sophisticated and Mafia-like smuggling economy, one that increasingly merges drug and migrant smuggling. Drugs are buried deep in difficult-to-inspect shipping cargo or conveyed through elaborate systems of tunnels under the wall. Approximately forty tunnels have been discovered at the U.S.-Mexico border since 2001, and twice that many have been found since the authorities began keeping records on them in 1990. Some include lights, drainage, ventilation systems, pulley operations for moving cargo, and connect warehouses on one side of the border to warehouses on the other.[7] In addition to tunnels, boats may be used in place of land routes, and smugglers have also been known to cut holes in less monitored parts of fences, which they often then gate and vigilantly police against use by other smugglers.[8] Third, and related, border intensifications and responses to them render the border zone itself an increasingly violent space. In the U.S. case, migrants are sometimes left by their smugglers to die of thirst and exposure in the desert or abandoned to suffocate in car trunks, vans, or trucks. Smugglers themselves are more often armed and violent: In 2007 alone, in California, there were 340 documented assaults on Border Patrol agents, who were attacked with weapons ranging from nail-studded planks to Molotov cocktails.[9] Meanwhile, border towns, once relatively peaceful, if impoverished and unhappy places, have become garrisons, complete with lookout towers for smugglers built on top of houses. The Border Patrol responds in turn with elaborate all-night floodlight systems, giving these towns the look of detention camps, and has also resorted to firing pepper spray and tear gas into the towns to rout smugglers.[10] In short, what prior to border fortifications was a more laconic and less dangerous cat-and-mouse game between the Border Patrol and illegals increasingly now resembles a scene of permanent guerilla warfare and counterinsurgency.

Border fortifications also multiply other outlaw elements. As Chapter 3 detailed, well-organized vigilante groups frustrated with state laxity or inefficacy undertake to police borders or assert jurisdictional sovereignty on their own. In the U.S. case, in addition to hunting down illegal crossers and thwarting the efforts of those who would abet them, this now includes armed invasions of the homes of alleged illegal immigrants: In May 2009, a man and his ten-year-old daughter were shot dead in their home by members of the Minutemen American Defense group. The group was seeking money and contraband to finance their vigilante activities.[11]

The state, too, is implicated in heightened lawlessness related to border space and activity. As Chapter 1 recounted, the Real ID Act of 2005 allowed the Department of Homeland Security to "waive any and all laws necessary to ensure expeditious construction of the barriers and roads," permitting the set-aside of laws ranging from environmental protocols to Native American protections.[12] The Secure Fence Act of 2006 permitted the direct violation of private-property rights to build the border barrier. While standing for law and order against violence and illegality, the wall not only generates violence and nonstate rogue actors, but licenses rogue state activity.

In short, where demand pulls the supply of labor or contraband and where state expansion and/or occupation is at stake, walls produce borders as permanent zones of violent conflict and lawlessness, incite sophisticated and dangerous underground industries, expand the size and expense of the problems they would solve, and aggravate hostilities on both sides. Most of the examples offered here have dwelt on the U.S.-Mexico wall, but it is easy enough to extend the analysis to other efforts at walling out the Third World, or to efforts, such as those in certain regions of Africa and South Asia, at walling out more poor from less poor parts of the world, or to walls staking claims where land jurisdiction is contested.

Why, then, build walls? What generates fierce popular passions for walling alongside state investments in these icons to and of failure — the failure of nation-state sovereignty. followed by the literal failure of the walls that would prop this faltering sovereignty? If one quasi-psychoanalytic answer suggests the "I know — but still..." structure of the fetish, that is, "I know they don't really work, but still, they satisfy," this poses the question of what desire the fetish is harboring. In a context of declining protective capacities of the state, diluted nationhood, and the increasing vulnerability of subjects everywhere to global economic vicissitudes and transnational violence, we need to understand the political wishes for potency, protection, containment, and even innocence that may be projected onto walls. We need to grasp what the new walls psychically address or assuage, even when they cannot deliver on their material promises.

Fantasies of Walled Democracy
In *Imagined Communities*, Benedict Anderson argues that nations are "imagined" as bounded, sovereign, and communal.[13] If boundary, sovereignty, and national community are precisely what globalization erodes, how might walls fictively restore these elements of a national imaginary? What kind of threatened or compromised identity, of subject or nation, is generating the desire for walling? In the context of an increasingly interdependent, unhorizoned, as well as openly inegalitarian global order, what do walls help to ward off psychically or repress, or what kind of psychic political defenses might walls emblematize? How might walls serve as a set of national psychic defenses, as prophylactics

against confrontation with our own ills or as projections onto others and onto an elsewhere of a nation's own needs, dependencies, and hungers? To this end, what political-economic logics do nation-state walls help to invert rhetorically or reverse such that the poor, the colonized, or the exploited can be figured as aggressors? And, as they resurrect myths of sovereign containment and protection, what fantasies of national purity and national innocence do they gratify?[14]

This chapter proceeds by first speculatively engaging these questions through consideration of four historically specific national fantasies. It then turns to psychoanalytic thought in an effort to deepen and ground these speculations.

The Fantasy of the Dangerous Alien
in an Increasingly Borderless World threatening

Associations of political outsiders with difference and danger are as old as human community itself. Demonizing constructions of tribal or political outsiders are widely recorded by anthropologists and political historians and appear as well in the etymologies of words such as "barbarian" and "alien," both of which were coined to name a particular other, but then became names for generic pejorative and threatening figures of otherness. Moreover, as Mary Douglas argues, border violations themselves are almost universally associated with pollution and danger.[15] Thus, as sovereignty weakens and borders are more routinely trespassed and as the nation itself loses clear definition, it is hardly surprising that the alien is drawn as an especially powerful and dangerous figure, even in the epoch of the global village. Perhaps more striking are the diverse elements that make up this composite portrait of danger.

In the U.S. post–Cold War context, the border has been discursively constructed as a point of entry for a variety of heterogeneous threats to the nation, threats increasingly merged into a single figure of alien danger. Tom Ridge, the first head of the U.S. Department of Homeland Security established in 2001, declared the border "a conduit for terrorists, weapons of mass destruction, illegal migrants, contraband, and other unlawful commodities." But it is a statement by Steven A. Camarota, director of research for the Center for Immigration Studies, an anti-immigration think tank, that exemplifies their conjoining: "We can't protect ourselves from terrorism," he proclaimed, "without dealing with illegal immigration."[16] Post-9/11 popular discourse, especially that arguing for completion of the border wall, also merges these threats: Campaigns on behalf of border fortifications in general and of walling in particular routinely identify unchecked illegal immigration with the danger of terrorism, despite little evidence of the connection.

The political, security, and economic effects of globalization, however, do not exhaust the elements animating contemporary First World constructions of a figure of alien enmity. There are also the challenges to hegemonic culture, language, and race posed by large numbers of immigrant Latinos in North America, Arabs in Europe, South Asians in Australia, and of course, Palestinians in Israel. For those of the hegemon, these challenges may be to both individual and national identity, the psychic and social "I" and "we" that the nation has long secured. Hence the repeated European uproars over Muslim dress codes and other cultural practices or the repeated bids for "English-only" voting materials and school curriculums in the United States. At the academic level, this threat to identity is formulated as a challenge to Western values by "immigrants from other civilizations [sic] who reject assimilation and continue to adhere to and to propagate the values, customs and cultures of their home societies."[17] When this rejection of Western values is affirmed and strengthened through the more general promulgation of multiculturalism in Western societies, Samuel Huntington adds, this "means effectively the end of Western civilization" and of the countries upholding it. "A country not belonging to any civilization [lacks] a cultural core. History shows that no country so constituted can long endure as a coherent society."[18] Western civilization and Western nations are not merely being culturally diluted or economically drained by immigrants, but sacked.

The figure of alien danger is thus literally overdetermined today, comprising economic, political, security, and cultural effects of globalization. These disparate elements are fused into one, producing "the alien" as a many-headed dragon. Of course this construction disavows the Northern demand for cheap, unprotected labor and the fact that most terrorist events in Europe and the United States have been homegrown. (In the United States, this includes the Weathermen, the Unabomber, Timothy McVeigh, who blew up the Oklahoma City Federal Building, and Bruce Ivins, the army microbiologist thought to be responsible for the September 2001 anthrax attacks, as well as a host of school and workplace shooters and bombers.) It occludes studies revealing that new immigrant neighborhoods have generally lower crime rates than other parts of Western nations.[19] And it occludes the mutable nature of culture and identity, that is, the extent to which cultures are not timeless and unchanging, but live in history and persist through transformation and the incorporation of new elements.

Importantly, the discourse of walling and the fantasy it holds out of being able to seal the nation off from the outside themselves facilitate these disavowals and occlusions. Walls are a scrim on which can be projected an anthropomorphized other as the cause of national woes ranging from dilutions of ethnicized national identity to drug use, crime, and declining real wages. The nation is under assault and needs to bunker itself against a "Third World invasion." In short, the bid for walls both emerges from and abets a discourse in which foreign labor, multiculturalism, and terrorism are merged and relocated from consequence to cause of the loosened enclosing folds of the nation and the growing limits on state protective capacities.

Fantasies of Containment

The projection of danger onto the alien both draws on and fuels a fantasy of containment for which walls are the ultimate icon.

117

The protective walls of the home are now extended to the nation, taking to a parodic height Hannah Arendt's argument in *The Human Condition* that the overtaking of the political by the social in modernity converts the nation into a giant household.[20]

In the face of an increasingly unbounded and uncontrolled global order, walls figure containment that exceeds mere protection against dangerous invaders and that pertains instead to the psychic unmanageability of living in such a world. The need for containment, at times depicted as the need for horizons, is a theme sounded frequently by nineteenth-century and early twentieth-century thinkers, albeit oddly, less often today. For Nietzsche, "a living thing can be healthy, strong and fruitful only when bounded by a horizon," and for psychoanalysis, loss of containment is a road to psychosis.[21] In his critique of the impulse to develop a "world picture," Heidegger writes, "shelter is provided by the horizon's ability to turn the threatening world of the 'outside' into a reassuring picture."[22] Walling phantasmatically produces such shelter when the actual boundaries of the nation cease to be containing, and it is noteworthy that merely "virtual fences," consisting of sensors and screening devices, are not up to the task. That is, walls—solid, visible walls—are demanded when the constitutive political horizon for the "we" and the "I" is receding.

If in a Westphalian order the state is the container for the nation and political sovereignty contributes the hard metal of this container, then it is unsurprising that contemporary nationalisms issue demands for rearticulated state sovereignty through visible signs of its containing powers.[23] Settled and intact state sovereignty does not require such signs. It produces bounded national composition and order without hyperbolic border militarization and barricading—it orders through its structuring and ubiquitous presence, through the charisma of sovereignty, and above all, through the fusion of nation, state, and sovereign. Waning state sovereignty loses these capacities to contain the nation and the subject. Thus does Achille Mbembe formulate the detachment of sovereignty from the state as an emasculation of the state, one that parallels the demasculinization of the male civil population in the decimation of familial patriarchalism. In the case of the postcolony, he adds, this demasculinization is compensated by phallic militarism, a literal fetishization of guns.[24] Walls appear to be a related fetish, one that similarly reaches from state to subject in promising restored potency.

Seen from a slightly different angle, the call for strong state iteration of national boundaries would be a crucial element in what Saskia Sassen terms the "renationalizing" of political discourse corresponding to denationalized economic space. Boundary iteration and defense stages the righteousness and the possibility of such renationalization against its contemporary undoing.[25] Thus do declining state sovereignty and the disappearing viability of a homogeneous national imaginary redress each other at the site of walls. Visible walls respond to the need for containment and boundaries in too global a world, too unhorizoned a universe. They produce a spatially demarcated "us," national identity, and national political scale when these can no longer be fashioned from conceits of national political or economic autonomy, demographic homogeneity, or shared history, culture, and values.

Fantasies of Impermeability
Containment within an increasingly boundaryless world is one kind of psychic longing animating the desire for walls; the fantasy of impermeability—perhaps even impenetrability—complements it. Sovereign power carries the fantasy of an absolute and enforceable distinction between inside and outside. This distinction in turn depends upon sovereignty's defiance of spatial or boundary porousness and of temporal interruption or multivalence. Political sovereignty, like that of God, entails absolute jurisdictional control and endurance over time. The sovereign can be attacked, but not penetrated without being undone, challenged, but not interrupted without being toppled. In this respect, sovereignty appears as a supremely masculine political fantasy (or fallacy)

of mastery: Penetration, pluralization, or interruption are its literal undoing.

It is significant, in this regard, that most discourses of walling in the United States, Europe, and Israel produce the entity at stake as simultaneously vulnerable, victimized, righteous, and powerful. The nation is in danger, under siege; the state is appealed to as capable of defending against this siege and eminently right to do so. Here it may be useful to remember that walls of premodern European cities were mainly built against sieges for plunder, not as fortresses against political-military conquest.[26] The siege was a routine economic phenomenon in the Middle Ages, and an entity "under siege" for economic plunder by a neighboring entity is in a different situation from one engaged in a political-territorial war, even as the siege may constitute an element in war tactics. The blending of military and economic elements in the siege facilitates an appreciation of how defenses against migrating peoples today so easily acquire a security aspect in contemporary walling discourse. Sieges work by penetrating defenses, swarming a defended area, and plundering its resources—exactly how "invading immigrant hordes" are frequently depicted in the Euro-Atlantic world today. Thus, a nation "under siege" justifies defenses and blockades even amid NAFTA-type agreements, on the one hand, and military (or terrorist) technologies that make walls irrelevant, on the other. Indeed, Palestinians flooding Egypt last year through the breached Gaza wall in order to purchase food, fuel, and other domestic necessities might be framed as a kind of siege in reverse, or perhaps as a specifically late capitalist siege in which a desperate need for access to cheap commodities, and not only to capital itself, is what "batters down Chinese walls."[27] Even terror, though not economically driven, may be more appropriately framed as siege, rather than as warfare—it aims at plunder, not sovereign conquest. Yet the siege, presumed to have passed from history with the emergence of the modern nation-state, is a relatively nontheorized phenomenon within liberalism. This is one reason why walls and their putative aims lack a lexicon or grammar in liberal theory, including in theories of international conflict.

The defense that walls establish against siege works the fantasy of impermeability into a psychic politics in which the enemy is figured as raiding, invading, coming to take or plunder what is rightfully the nation's own—its safety, security, peaceful or prosperous way of life, its jobs, its wealth, its First World privilege, its civilized existence or liberal democratic values. As I will suggest next, this enemy also tears at First World subjects' psychic political insulation from the hierarchies and violence in the global webs of dependency sustaining them. Walls are a visual means of restoring this psychic insulation. They help to restore images of national self-sufficiency, and they help to screen out suffering or destitution.

Fantasies of Purity, Innocence, and Goodness
"Saving Lives—Israel's Anti-Terrorist Fence: Answers to Questions" is an Israeli government public-relations document written in English—clearly for American and European consumption—that gently rebukes criticisms of the Wall and calmly explains its rationale. The document depicts the barrier as a fence, rather than a wall ("97% of the fence is not concrete," it notes repeatedly), as apolitical and unrelated to the question of negotiating a settlement or boundaries, as temporary and moveable in accord with negotiations and an end to Palestinian violence, and as built entirely on the humanitarian grounds of preserving and nurturing life. It presents both the policy architects and the contractors building the wall as deeply concerned with human life and livelihoods on both sides of the barrier. All involved, the document reports, have been careful to treat Palestinians, their lands, and their villages with respect and care. The rationale for the Wall itself is similarly framed: Israel is a tiny, humane, democratic nation victimized by barbaric neighbors who must be walled out unless or until they change their terrible ways.[28] The wall, in short, is depicted as preserving innocence and civilization against its opposite and as standing in every way for humane

and life-preserving values against barbaric and murderous ones.

The many Web sites devoted to justifying and promoting the U.S.-Mexico wall are similar, if generally less sophisticated and less defensive.[29] Porous borders, the story goes, permit the flow of drugs, crime, and terror into a civilized nation whose only crime is to have been too prosperous, generous, tolerant, open, and free. In both the U.S. and Israeli cases, walling expresses and gratifies this desire for a national imago of goodness, one that wholly externalizes the nation's ills and disavows its unlovely effects on others, its aggressions, needs, and dependencies. In this regard, the desire for walling responds to a historical moment in which structural inequalities and dependencies (between Global North and Global South, rich and poor, settler and native, white and colored) have been both spatially desegregated and challenged as natural or legitimate, but are not thereby undone. That is, at the same time that racialized discourses justifying colonialism, natural hierarchies, and global inequalities have lost their easy hegemony, global movements of people and capital have eroded the separate spheres inhabited by the populations these stratifications produce. Today, rich and poor, colonizer and native, First and Third World live virtually and actually in ever greater proximity. The result is a world of extreme and intimate inequality deprived of strong legitimating discourses—apart from neoliberalism's giant "whatever" shrug.

For the predicament this condition produces for those wanting to understand themselves as justice-minded and good, or at least innocent, walling offers several discursive exits. Mobilized to depict discursively what it blocks as lawless invaders, walling literally screens out a confrontation with global inequality or local colonial domination. It facilitates denial of the dependency of the privileged on the exploited and of the agency of the dominant in producing the resistance of the oppressed. Two Israeli anti-Wall activists develop this point, arguing that the Wall's "ugliness" is essential, rather than incidental, functioning as a theater of ugliness projected onto the other:

122

The wall allows Israel not to see itself as aggressive, violent, cruel, possessive, a violator of human rights, by projecting all these traits on the Palestinians beyond the wall. The wall is not perceived by [Zionists] as an aggressive act; it is perceived as a protective act, an act of self-defense.... It takes a complex psychological mechanism to facilitate such a reversal.... The wall achieves its goal: protecting Israel from seeing its own aggression and thus preserving its basic assumption that it is the "good" "just" victim.[30]

Figuring what is outside as invading, but also literally blocking from view the often impoverished conditions that they block out, late modern walls facilitate a conversion of subordination and exploitation into a dangerous threat neither produced by nor connected to the needs of the dominant. Rewriting dependency as autonomy, walling in this context displaces appreciation of webs of social relations with the fiction of autarky. Optically and psychically, at the moment that global demographics and economics undermine ontologized political and economic identities, walling resurrects ontological ascriptions of (victimized) goodness to the dominant and (agentic) hostility, violence, knavery or greed to the subordinate.

The Psychoanalysis of Defense

In order to provide something of an analytic firmament for these speculations about desires for walling, we turn now to two strands of psychoanalytic theory. The first is the theory of defense offered in early papers by Sigmund Freud and extended by Anna Freud in *The Ego and Mechanisms of Defense*. The second is Sigmund Freud's account of the origin and persistence of religion in *The Future of an Illusion*.

Sigmund Freud's Early Theory of Defense

At first blush, Freud's theory of defense in two papers, "Neuro-Psychoses of Defense" and "Further Thoughts on the Neuro-Psychoses of Defense," would not seem to have an immediate bearing on the desire for walling. This is both because Freud is primarily concerned with defenses against unbidden sexual desires and because he conceives defenses as ways of rerouting or avoiding conscious confrontation with such desires, rather than as simple psychic barriers or fortresses. Yet if Freud's arguments are deliteralized, detached from exclusive concern with sexuality, and considered closely, we may discover something quite useful here.

In his two papers on defense, Freud says defenses arise in response to anxiety about something distressing. (He calls this distressing something an "idea," although the idea constitutes the ideational version, even compression, of a desire or experience.) Freud posits a dialectical relation between defense and repression: On the one hand, defense entails repression of the distressing material, while on the other, repression itself is a form of defense. This is important because the defense is not aimed only at the idea, but also at its energy — defense is the means by which the source, content, *and* energy of the anxiety are repressed. That is, the ego defends itself not just against content, but against the energy or affect of the unwanted content. This is how repression is both a psychic act and a psychic effect.[31]

Let us rehearse the logic here: "Defense hysteria," Freud says, is unique. It differs from what he calls "hypnoid" and "retention" hysteria because it involves attempting to *deny or repel* a distressing experience/idea/desire that produces a contradiction or shock for the ego.[32] The task that the ego sets is to make the incompatible idea *"non arrivée"* — not to have come at all. The task is first carried out by turning the powerful idea into a weak one, which is accomplished through "conversion" of the idea into an obsession of some sort "which lodges in consciousness like a parasite." But if a fresh impression like the original "breaks through the barrier erected by the will," the weakened idea is furnished with fresh affect, so a further conversion is needed, which ultimately takes hold as a defense. Even when successful, however, this resolution is unstable, giving rise to episodic hysterical attacks. And if conversion is not possible, then the idea is fended off only by separating it from its affect, and obsessions or

phobias "unrelated to reality" will result. The obsession or phobia, Freud says, is a substitute or surrogate for the incompatible
idea and takes its place in consciousness.[33]

So Freud identifies two possibilities for the ego's response
to unacceptable desire. There is either complete conversion to
another idea (defense), which, while producing periodic hysterical outbursts, wholly suppresses the original anxiety, or there is
conversion of the unacceptable desire's energy into an obsession
or phobia. Both possibilities, he insists, are modalities of protecting the ego against ideas that conflict with its notion of itself.

The unacceptable ideas producing the desire for walling and
generating hysteria about permeability, immigrants, or even terror may not be limited to immediate desires from within the
entity doing the walling. Instead they may pertain to one or more
of the following difficult-to-accept and even frightening features
of contemporary existence: the limited capacity for (economic,
cultural, and even legal) containment exercised by the nation-
state today; the weakening of sovereign protective capacities; the
declining power and supremacy of the Euro-Atlantic world and
the attendant loss of status for the working and middle classes; the
erosion of national identity based on a shared language and culture; the reliance of Euro-Atlantic prosperity on the production
of an impoverished outside; perhaps above all, a Euro-Atlantic
existence full of crime, drugs, violence, ennui, depression and
drained of its secure economic might, social stability, political
power, and cultural supremacy. The hysterical obsession is The
Alien, fashioned as a single imaginary creature from the material
of immigrants, drug traffickers, and terrorists and representing
the pollution of violated borders and the demasculinization of
permeable national and individual subjecthood. The phobia is
xenophobia. Thus do walls conceived to block danger discursively
produce it. At the same time, walls facilitate a psychic defense
against recognition of a set of internal or systemic failures that
are relocated to the outside and against recognition of a set of
unacceptable facts of dependency, unprotected vulnerability, or

even responsibility for colonial violence in the context of declining sovereign power. Walling makes recognition of these failures
and facts "*non arrivée*," just as it literally aims to make migrants
and terrorists *non arrivée*. Moreover, building the walls themselves becomes obsessional, as the Minutemen's tracking of illegal
entrants is obsessional. The convergence of unprotected vulnerability resulting from sovereign decline amid global markets and
global terror produces a national egoic response that seeks literal
defenses to prop up psychic ones or that spurs the construction of
literal defenses in the production of psychic ones.

Anna Freud's Elaboration of the Theory of Defense
In *The Ego and Mechanisms of Defense*, Freud's daughter, Anna,
sought to systematize and scientize her father's theory of defense.
While the elder Freud is often thought to have replaced the notion
of defense with the notion of repression, Anna Freud claims that
repression actually "ends up being only a special mechanism of
defense," one that protects the ego against instinctual demands,
while defense has a significantly broader range.[34] In fact, Anna
Freud argues, there are ten distinct mechanisms of defense:
regression, repression, reaction formation, isolation, undoing, projection, introjection, turning against the self/subject,
reversal, and sublimation.[35] These may operate separately or in
clusters; different mechanisms are triggered by different kinds
of anxieties and according to other elements in the personality.

For our purposes, Anna Freud's most important hypotheses
are these: First, the defense of repression is most valuable for
combating sexual wishes, while other defense mechanisms better
serve other instinctual forces, especially aggressive impulses.[36]
Second, anxiety is always what sets the defensive process into
motion. This anxiety can be a superegoic response to the id's
desires, a response to objectively frightening or disturbing
things in the world, or an egoic response to the sheer strength of
instincts.[37] Third, defenses are always built against the impulse
and the affect of the anxiety; they are never merely against certain

126

ideas.[38] Finally, defenses are designed to secure the ego and save it from experiencing pain — again, a pain that may arise from within or come from the outside world.[39]

With the first and second points, Anna Freud opens out the operation of defense beyond sexual anxiety. She stresses the importance of building defenses against anxieties whose source ranges from intolerable internal psychic aggression to a frightening aspect of the external world. With the third point, she argues that defenses address and redirect affect, not just ideas. Consequently, the whole personality can be transformed by defense, and it is this transformation that allows us to speak of "character defense" in a particular person. With the fourth point, Anna Freud underscores the two primary purposes of defense: stabilizing the ego and securing it from internal and external sources of suffering. All of these points are also reminders that while defenses can arise episodically and in response to contingent impulses or experiences, they are most significant as enduring aspects of subject formation and, as such, produce their own train of additional effects on the subject.

Before drawing these elements of psychoanalytic defense theory toward the desire for walling, I want to highlight one rhetorical aspect of this theory as it is elaborated by both father and daughter, namely, its heavy reliance on spatial and especially military metaphors. We already glimpsed this reliance in Sigmund Freud's early papers where he discussed barriers, separations, and the interdiction of would-be arrivals. Now consider the way that Anna Freud sets up the whole problem of defenses:

> On their way to gratification, the id-impulses must pass through the territory of the ego and here they are in an alien atmosphere.... [The id's] instinctual impulses continue to pursue their aims with their own peculiar tenacity and energy, and they make hostile incursions into the ego, and in the hope of overthrowing it by a surprise attack. The ego on its side becomes suspicious; it proceeds to counter-attack and to invade the territory of the id. Its purpose is to

put the instincts permanently out of action by means of appropriate defensive measures, designed to secure its own boundaries.... No longer do we see an undistorted id-impulse but an id-impulse modified by some defensive measure on the part of the ego.[40]

Anna Freud formulates the id-ego relation as a protracted struggle over territorial domain and boundaries, complete with incursions, attacks, counterattacks, defenses, and border fortifications. She also constructs this theater of struggle as that through which self and other, identity and alien, are performatively brought into being and negotiated. Her basic account of the psyche recalls Carl Schmitt's insistence in *Nomos of the Earth* that in the beginning (of all law and hence peoplehood) was land appropriation.[41] Yet she also postulates inevitable boundary breaches—the impulses of the id, she says, must pass through the territory of the ego—which produce the necessity of defense and transform both the transgressor and the transgressed. The landscape she describes is one of permanent hostilities, territorially motivated attacks and counterattacks, the production of defensive measures against threats to identity through which identity is also produced and hardened. This territorial struggle all takes place within the subject—it is an intrapsychic battle for the identity of the subject.

What does the ego, the conscious "*moi*," become consequent to these battles? "The defended ego," Anna Freud says, "takes the form of bodily attitudes such as stiffness and rigidity, a fixed smile, contempt, irony, and/(or) arrogance."[42] Defense paradoxically produces a fragility and brittleness, what, borrowing from Wilhelm Reich, Anna Freud identifies as the "armor plating of character," which, again, more than merely attaching to the ego, transforms it. Hegel's shadow is discernible here as defenses come to reduce the resilience, adeptness, and flexibility—the powers—of the entity they are built to secure. (Consider this paradoxical effect in the state of Israel today.) Moreover, the ego thus constructed will inevitably block not only untoward impulses or experiences, but *analysis itself*, where analysis stands not simply

for formal psychoanalytic work, but for all forms of self-reflex-
ivity. The ego comes to be defined by these defenses, and not
merely protected by them. Consequently, it fiercely resists submitting them to critical undoing.[43]

Now let us see what the two Freuds' accounts of defense might
contribute to theorizing the late modern desire for walls. If psychic defenses are always attempts to shield the subject from pain
issuing either from external sources or from its own unacceptable
energies, the new nation-state walls may be seen to function in
precisely this way. Defenses, the Freuds argue, spare the ego from
any encounter that disturbs the ego's conceit of itself. This includes
blocking encounters with the id's own aggression or hostility, a
blocking that allows the ego to split off from the id to construct
an identity of virtue and goodness. Translated into the desire for
walling, national identity is restored not only to potency, but to
virtue through walls. It is cleansed of both its identification and its
imbrication with what it is walling out, whether extreme global
inequalities, capital's demand for cheap illegal labor, or anticolonial rage. Thus do walls help to defend the identity, virtue, and
strength of the nation against a variety of challenges.

Rhetorically, the spectacle of the wall reverses and displaces a
range of disturbances to national identity, from disavowed predicates of its existence to the "strength of its own instincts," that
is, its own aggressions toward what it is walling out.[44] As "efforts
by the ego to repudiate part of its own id," walls help to protect
(and hence to produce) a national ego/identity—fortifying its
boundaries and suppressing its predicates. These include, in the
U.S. case, various effects of neoliberal globalization that together
degrade the boundaries and ethnic-cultural homogeneity of the
nation and that also affront its conceits of equality, universality,
and fairness. Mobilizing the defenses that Anna Freud names
"reversal" and "displacement," walls against immigration con-
strue it as an invasion, rather than a global production, especially
insofar as they rearticulate in spatial terms an outmoded sense of
nation and belonging.[45]

The Israeli wall does something similar, albeit with the colonial native, rather than the laborer, figured as persecutor or invader. Emanating from and contributing to a discourse of Israel's singular civility in a barbarous environment — "a villa in a jungle,"[46] as Ehud Barak has called it — the Wall abets discursive reversal of the fount of aggression generating the enmity it would repel. Producing as well an ever more militarized and checkpointed order of existence for all (Palestinian-Israeli MP Azmi Bishara refers to Israel as "the state of the checkpoints" and Palestine as "the land of the checkpoints"), the Wall itself hardens Israel's defensive, besieged, and defended condition into identity and character inside and out.[47]

Viewed as a form of national psychic defense, walls can be seen as an ideological disavowal of a set of unmanageable appetites, needs, and powers. They facilitate a set of metalepses in which the specter of invasion replaces internal need or desire and the specter of violent hostility replaces reckoning with colonial displacements and occupation. Through their ostentatious signification of sovereign power and definition of the nation, they also deflect anxieties about the disintegration of national identity and about the decline of state sovereignty.[48] Indeed, they spectacularize a hyperidentity of the nation in response to anxiety about the detachment of sovereignty from the nation-state and globalization's dilution of homogeneous national cultures. In the language of Guy Debord, the spectacle is "a *Weltanschauung* that has been actualized, translated into the material real — a world view transformed into an objective force."[49]

One important omission from the Freuds' account of defense, of course, is the gendered dimensions of the anxieties these defenses are managing. There is a notably gendered inflection to walling as a defense against anxieties about need, vulnerability, and penetrability and to the desire for sovereign containment and protection against such vulnerability. Vulnerability and penetrability are almost universally coded as feminine; sovereign supremacy and powers of containment and protection are coded masculine. The desire for walling may emanate in part from a wish to be relieved of a feminized national subject condition and emasculated state power and also from an identification with sovereign political power, an identification facilitated by the circuitry between sovereign subject and sovereign state in liberalism discussed in Chapter 2. More generally, in a late modern context, walling appears to defend against a sovereign failure to protect a penetrable (penetrated) nation (always referred to with a feminine pronoun), a failure and penetration that also threatens to expose national dependencies and needfulness. The heterosexual coupling of the feminized nation and the masculinized sovereign state is no minor matter here. Absent the protection of a sovereign state, the nation stands vulnerable, violable, and desperate. Walling restores an imago of the sovereign and his protective capacities.

Illusions of a Future

By way of conclusion, we turn from Freud's thinking about defense to Freud's reflections on the human need for religion. This strand of Freud's thinking contributes to an appreciation of the theological dimension of sovereignty articulated most famously by Schmitt. Insisting that all political concepts descend from theology, Schmitt formulates political sovereignty as imitating God's power—supreme and temporally infinite. Chapters 2 and 3 argued that the theological face of state sovereignty reappears strongly at the moment of its waning. This is the argument I want to press through Freud's reflections on the origin and persistence of religion.

In *The Future of an Illusion*, Freud follows other nineteenth-century German critics of religion (most notably Feuerbach, but also Nietzsche, Marx, and Weber) in arguing that religion arises from an unbearable experience of human vulnerability and dependency in both the natural and social world. Freud's distinctive contribution to this critique formulates this vulnerability as taking the psychic form of "infantile helplessness." Religious ideation, Freud argues, is a reaction not merely to ubiquitous human vulnerability, but to the particular resonance this vulnerability has with the experience of infancy. Man's terrible vulnerability to fate, suffering, and the forces of nature resonates psychically with the infant's absolute inability to care for itself and its radical dependency on others who may hurt or terrify it, as well as protect it. According to Freud, religious ideation will recapitulate this experience, meaning that God will be cast in the image of all-powerful parents.[50] The human artifact of religion thus produces a God who is at once frightening and loving: God replicates the unique dual character of parents as sources of absolute fear and absolute protection. Religion acknowledges our helplessness, Freud says, even as it is a strategy to overcome the humiliation of that helplessness with an anthropomorphized figure of protection.

Armed with this understanding of religion's psychic origin and function, Freud believes he can explain a fundamental conundrum of a scientific age, namely, why religion persists even after reason and science should have discredited and displaced it. Religion does not collapse so easily for a very specific reason. It is not merely an error, but an illusion, Freud argues—the important distinction being that errors are mistakes, while an illusion is powered by a wish.[51] The wish for sovereign protection that generates and sustains religion is so powerful and emerges from such a primal psychic experience that it cannot be addressed by any other force or allayed by science or reason. Hence, religion will not die upon being disproved.[52]

How does Freud's argument bear on the contemporary phenomenon of walling? To the extent that walls optically gratify the wish for intact sovereign power and protection, to the extent that they produce an imago of such power and protection and an effect of sovereign awe, the desire for walling appears as a religiously inflected one. It is a desire that recalls the theological dimension of political sovereignty. So, too, does the notion of sealing ourselves off from a dangerous outside appear animated by a yearning to resolve the vulnerability and helplessness produced by myriad global forces and flows coursing through nations today. The fantasy that the state can and will provide this resolution thus reconvenes a strong religious version of state sovereignty. The desire for national walling carries this theological wish, and walls themselves may visually gratify it.

Ancient temples housed gods within an unhorizoned and overwhelming landscape. Nation-state walls are modern-day temples housing the ghost of political sovereignty. They organize deflection from crises of national cultural identity, from colonial domination in a postcolonial age, and from the discomfort of privilege obtained through superexploitation in an increasingly interconnected and interdependent global political economy. They confer magical protection against powers incomprehensibly large, corrosive, and humanly uncontrolled, against reckoning with the effects of a nation's own exploits and aggressions, and against dilution of the nation by globalization. These theological and psychological features of the clamor for walls help explain why their often enormous costs and limited efficacy are irrelevant to the desire for them. They produce not the future of an illusion, but the illusion of a future aligned with an idealized past. Sigmund Freud will have the last words here: "We call a belief an illusion when a wish-fulfillment is prominent in its motivation, and in doing so we disregard its relations to reality, just as the illusion itself sets no store by verification.... Having recognized religious doctrines as illusions, we are at once faced by a further question.... Must not the assumptions that determine our political regulations be called illusions as well?"[53]

Acknowledgments

Many audiences and seminar participants around the globe responded to portions of this work over the past several years. Those who placed references in my hands, told me stories, sent me pictures, and supplemented my analyses gave me much; so also did those who argued with me or corrected my facts. The fine graduate research assistants who contributed to this project include Sarah Alexander, Ivan Ascher, Jack Jackson, Mi Lee, and Megan Wachspress. At Zone Books, Ramona Naddaff offered superb suggestions for revisions, Bud Bynack's copy-editing smoothed the prose, and Meighan Gale gave every aspect of production her expert hand and eye. A University of California President's Humanities Fellowship and a Humanities Research Fellowship from Berkeley enabled the book's completion.

Notes

CHAPTER ONE: WANING SOVEREIGNTY, WALLED DEMOCRACY

1. Elbit, the largest nongovernmental defense company in Israel, which is building the Israeli wall, was awarded a contract in 2006 to join with Boeing in constructing the wall on the Mexican border. *Jerusalem Post*, September 22, 2006, available on-line at http://www.jpost.com/servlet/Satellite?pagename =JPost%2FJPArticle%2FShowFull&cid=1157913683759 (last accessed October 6, 2009). Transnational links have also developed between resistance movements and especially with regard to mural work at the two sites: A Palestinian group recently invited Mexican mural artists who have produced protest art on the Mexican wall to paint on the Israeli wall.

2. Rama Lakshmi, "India's Border Fence Extended to Kashmir: Country Aims to Stop Pakistani Infiltration," *Washington Post*, July 30, 2003; "Border Jumpers: The World's Most Complex Borders: Pakistan/India," *PBS: Wide-angle*, available on-line at http://www.pbs.org/wnet/wideangle/episodes/ border-jumpers/the-worlds-most-complex-borders/pakistanindia/2340 (last accessed October 6, 2009).

3. Alissa J. Rubin, "Outcry over Wall Shows Depth of Iraqi Resentment," News Analysis, *New York Times,* April 23, 2007.

4. This pattern of stratified flows through variegated openings in the new barriers extends from expedited airport security processing for business-class and first-class passengers to the differential entry procedures for travelers crossing the U.S. borders from Canada and Mexico and for those crossing from the Palestinian territories into Israel. See Matthew Sparke, "A Neoliberal Nexus: Economy, Security, and the Biopolitics of Citizenship of the Border,"

Political Geography (January 2006), for a thoughtful discussion of the expedited border crossing program called "NEXUS and other so-called Smart Border programs which exemplify how a business class civil citizenship has been extended across transnational space at the very same time as economic liberalization and national securitization have curtailed citizenship for others" (p. 1).

5. The decline of nation-state sovereignty amid globalization, on the one hand, and of individual sovereignty amid unprecedentedly dense social powers constructing, regulating, and buffeting the subject, on the other, together mark the waning of sovereignty respectively identified with Westphalia (the articulation of an order based on sovereign nation-states), the French Revolution (the inauguration of popular sovereignty), and Kant (the articulation of the sovereign moral subject). Indeed, one reason that sovereignty has mostly lain dormant in political theory from the late eighteenth century until very recently, when an extraordinary range of thinkers has taken it up, pertains to this waning. As Hegel would have it, sovereignty becomes a theoretical preoccupation as its distinctly modern form is dying.

6. In chapter 8 of the first book of *République*, Jean Bodin identifies sovereignty as "the absolute and perpetual power of a commonwealth . . . the highest power of command," a formulation Schmitt shares and sharpens. But in chapter 10, Bodin's account shifts to "marks of sovereignty," a move that emphasizes the importance of reading sovereignty through its attributes and activities, rather than through abstract essential qualities. Among these marks: to give orders, but not receive them; to make, repeal, and interpret laws; to administer justice; to make or change judgments; to pardon; to coin money; to tax; to raise armies; and to make agreements or war with other rulers. See Jean Bodin, *On Sovereignty,* trans. and ed. Julian Franklin (Cambridge: Cambridge University Press, 1992), chs. 8 and 10.

7. Some thinkers have argued that international human rights promotion can and ought to strengthen, rather than weaken nation-state sovereignty, arguing that "national constitutional regimes represent the best guarantee of human rights." Michael Ignatieff, *Human Rights as Politics and Idolatry* (Princeton, NJ: Princeton University Press, 2001), p. 35.

8. Mike Davis refers to the triple layers of steel wall at the San Diego/San Ysidro portion of the U.S.-Mexico border as a "hyperbolic assertion of nation-state sovereignty." Mike Davis, "The Great Wall of Capital," in Michael

Sorkin (ed.), *Against the Wall: Israel's Barrier to Peace* (New York: New Press, 2005), p. 88.

9. Foucault writes: "Power relations are both intentional and nonsubjective. If in fact they are intelligible, this is not because they are the effect of another instance that 'explains' them, but rather because they are imbued, through and through, with calculation: There is no power that is exercised without a series of aims and objectives. But this does not mean that it results from the choice or decision of an individual subject; let us not look for the headquarters that presides over its rationality.... The logic is perfectly clear, the aims decipherable, and yet it is often the case that no one is there to have invented them, and few who can be said to have formulated them." *History of Sexuality, Volume 1: An Introduction*, trans. Robert Hurley (New York: Random House, 1978), pp. 94–95.

10. Such assertions are an important part of the art and value of theory, and there is nothing to apologize for here. Elsewhere, I have argued that theory depicts a world that does not quite exist, a world that is not quite the one we inhabit. See "At the Edge: The Future of Political Theory," in *Edgework* (Princeton, NJ: Princeton University Press, 2005), p. 80. An interval between the actual and the theoretical is crucial insofar as theory does not simply decipher the world, but recodes it in order to reveal something of the meanings and incoherencies with which we live. This is not simply to say that political and social theory describe reality abstractly. At their best, they conjure relations and meanings that illuminate the real or that help us recognize the real, but this occurs in grammars and formulations other than those of the real.

11. This last was suggested by Eyal Weizman in "The Wall and the Eye," an interview with Sina Najafi and Jeffrey Kastner, *Cabinet Magazine* 9 (Winter 2002), p. 31.

12. The practices of demographic separation within the context of colonial occupation, rather than institutionalized racism, are what make the analogy with South African apartheid relevant today. As Neve Gordon writes: "For many years... the occupation operated according to the colonization principle, by which I mean the attempt to administer the lives of the people and normalize the colonization, while exploiting the territory's resources (in this case land, water and labor). Over time, a series of structural contradictions undermined this principle and gave way in the mid-1990s to another guiding principle,

namely, the separation principle. By separation I mean the abandonment of efforts to administer the lives of the colonized population...while insisting on the continued exploitation of nonhuman resources (land and water). The lack of interest in or indifference to the lives of the colonized population that is characteristic of the separation principle accounts for the recent surge in lethal violence." Neve Gordon, *Israel's Occupation* (Berkeley: University of California Press, 2008), p. xix. For differences between apartheid in South Africa and the regime in the Occupied Palestinian Territories, see Hilla Dayan in "Principles of Old and New Regimes of Separation: Apartheid and Contemporary Israel/ Palestine," in Adi Ophir, Michal Givoni, and Sari Hanafi (eds.), *The Power of Inclusive Exclusion: Anatomy of Israeli Rule in the Occupied Palestinian Territories* (New York: Zone Books, 2009).

13. Quoted in *ibid.*, p. 197.

14. This variation corresponds to its varying appellations. The Wall is named the "security fence" or "peace wall" by its proponents, the "wall of shame" or "apartheid wall" by its opponents.

15. Randal C. Archibold, "New Fence Will Split a Border Park," *New York Times*, October 22, 2008, available on-line at http://www.nytimes. com/2008/10/22/us/22border.html; Dan Glaister, "Administration Moves to Bypass Laws to Complete Mexico Border Fence this Year," *Guardian Unlimited*, April 1, 2008, available on-line at http://www.guardian.co.uk/world/2008/ apr/01/usa.mexico (both last accessed October 13, 2009).

16. Eyal Weizman, *Hollow Land: Israel's Architecture of Occupation* (London: Verso, 2007), p. 177.

17. Weizman, *Hollow Land*, p. 173. There are also moveable stretches of the U.S.-Mexico border barrier: These sections of fencing sit on sand dunes and "float" with the shifting sands. When winds pile sand up against and on top of them, they can be scooped up, shaken off, and repositioned by all-terrain vehicles fitted with machines designed for the purpose. See "Floating Fence Helps Border Patrol," available on-line at http://www.kyma.com/ slp.php?idN=1916&cat=Local%20News. For commentary on the "floating fence," see http://subtopia.blogspot.com/2009/03/floating-fences-1-imperial-county.html (both last accessed October 13, 2009).

18. Azoulay and Ophir, "The Monster's Tail," in Sorkin (ed.), *Against the Wall*, p. 22.

19. *Ibid.*, p. 10.

20. *Hollow Land*, p. 179. Weizman also writes: "Although none of the maps released by the media or independent rights organizations actually show it, and all photographs of it depict a linear object resembling a border (and which all foreigners from territorially defined nation-states will immediately understand as such), the Wall has in fact become a discontinuous and fragmented series of self-enclosed barriers that can be better understood as a prevalent 'condition' of segregation.... With the rapid multiplication of 'depth barriers' the face of the territory has grown to resemble maps more redolent of Scandinavian coast-lines, where fjords, islands and lakes make an inconclusive separation between water and land" (p. 177).

21. *Ibid.*, p.172.

22. Stephen Farrell and Alissa J. Rubin, "As Fears Ease, Baghdad Sees Walls Tumble," *New York Times*, October 10, 2008, available on-line at http://www.nytimes.com/2008/10/10/world/middleeast/10walls.html (last accessed October 13, 2009). The first part of this article celebrates the removal of the giant cement slabs "the height of a double-decker bus" as "the most visible sign of a fundamental change here in the Iraqi capital," but the article later makes two confessions. First, "the walls are not coming down in all, or even most, Baghdad districts...they still surround the Green Zone, the once notori-ous airport highway, government buildings, checkpoints and entire neighbor-hoods," and second, "as they are removed, the bullet-pocked slabs are stacked in large storage zones waiting to be used elsewhere."

23. In a recent academic debate about immigration, Jean Bethke Elshtain argued that the difference between her own immigrant grandparents and con-temporary immigrants is that the former came to America because of its values, while the latter are concerned only with bettering their economic chances. Both the distinction and the veracity of the ascriptions are quite questionable. See "The Sheer Length of Stay Is Not By Itself Decisive" (Response to Joseph Carens), *Boston Review* (May/June, 2009).

24. Such, for example, is the case with what Weizman has named the "politics of verticality." See Eyal Weizman, "Introduction to the Politics of Verticality," available on-line at http://www.opendemocracy.net/conflict-politicsverticality/article_801.jsp (last accessed December 21, 2009).

25. Blas Nuñez-Neto and Yule Kim, "Border Security: Barriers Along the

U.S. International Border," Congressional Research Service Report for Congress, updated May 13, 2008, p. 7.

26. Dave Montgomery, "Border Fence Target: 300 Miles in 8 Months," *Fort Worth Star-Telegram*, April 27, 2008.

27. Nuñez-Neto and Kim, "Border Security," p. 33.

28. Although rarely read this way, nothing makes clearer how irrelevant the barrier is to overall migration rates than the severe drop in this rate during the recession commencing in 2008. A study published in May 2009 revealed that "the net outflow of migrants from Mexico—those who left minus those who returned—fell by about half in the year that ended in August 2008 from the preceding year." As demographer Jeffrey S. Pasel says, "If jobs are available, people come. If jobs are not available, people don't come." Cited in Julia Preston, "Mexican Data Show Migration to U.S. in Decline," *New York Times*, May 15, 2009, available on-line at http://www.nytimes.com/2009/05/15/us/15immig.html?scp=1&sq=recession,%20decrease,%20illegal,%20Mexico&st=cse (last accessed October 13, 2009).

29. Joseph Nevins, *Operation Gatekeeper: The Rise of the "Illegal Alien" and the Making of the U.S.-Mexico Boundary* (New York: Routledge, 2002), ch. 6, esp. pp. 124–30. See also Nuñez-Neto and Kim, "Border Security," pp. 40–41.

30. Paul Hirst, *Space and Power: Politics, War and Architecture* (Cambridge: Polity, 2005), p. 171.

31. Roxanne Panchasi, *Future Tense: The Culture of Anticipation in France Between the World Wars* (Ithaca, NY: Cornell University Press, 2009), pp. 88–91.

32. Greg Eghigian, "Homo Munitus," in Paul Betts and Katherine Pence (eds.), *Socialist Modern: East German Everyday Culture and Politics* (Ann Arbor: University of Michigan Press, 2008), pp. 43–44.

33. *Ibid.*, p. 10.

34. *Ibid.*, p. 6. For a discussion of the Western figure of this subject, see chapter 6 of Wendy Brown, *Regulating Aversion: Tolerance in the Age of Identity and Empire* (Princeton, NJ: Princeton University Press, 2007).

CHAPTER TWO: SOVEREIGNTY AND ENCLOSURE

A portion of this chapter was previously published in *The New Pluralism: William Connolly and the Contemporary Global Condition*, eds. David Campbell and Morton Schoolman (Durham, NC: Duke University Press, 2008).

1. Jost Trier, "Zaun und Manring," in *Beitragen zur Geschichte der deutschen Sprache und Literatur* 66 (1943): 232, cited in Carl Schmitt, *Nomos of the Earth in the International Law of the Jus Publicum Europaeum*, trans. G. L. Ulmen (New York: Telos Press, 2006), p. 75.

2. Jean-Jacques Rousseau, "Discourse on the Origins and Foundations of Inequality among Men," in *The First and Second Discourses*, ed. Roger D. Masters, trans. Roger D. Masters and Judith R. Masters (New York: St. Martin's Press, 1964), p. 141.

3. With his notion of the "politics of verticality," Eyal Weizman argues that currently in the West Bank, "sovereign relations are attempting to play themselves out three-dimensionally . . . obviously an unworkable absurdity." He goes on: "peace technicians—the people who are always drawing new maps for a solution—arrive at completely insane proposals for solving the problems of international boundaries in three dimensions. . . . Jerusalem itself, according to the Clinton plan, would have had 64 kilometers of walls and 40 bridges and tunnels connecting the enclaves to each other. . . . This is the total collapse of the idea of territory as produced by maps." Eyal Weizman, "The Wall and the Eye," an interview with Sina Najafi and Jeffrey Kastner, *Cabinet Magazine* 9 (Winter 2002), p. 31.

4. John Locke, *Second Treatise on Government*, in John Locke, *Two Treatises of Government: A Critical Edition With an Introduction and Apparatus Criticus*, ed. Peter Laslett (Cambridge: Cambridge University Press, 1963), para. 3, p. 308.

5. Schmitt, *Nomos of the Earth*, p. 47.

6. Locke, *Second Treatise*, paras. 108 and 359–60. In a brilliant qualifying exam essay Mi Lee brought to my attention the ubiquitous metaphor of fencing in Locke's *Second Treatise*. See *Second Treatise*, paras. 17, 93, 136, and esp. 222 and 226.

7. *Ibid.*, pp. 46 and 48.

8. *Ibid.*, pp. 70 and 74.

9. See Chris Fynsk's quarrel with Schmitt's account of *nomos*, "A *Nomos* without Truth," *South Atlantic Quarterly* 104, no. 2 (Spring 2005): pp. 313–17. I would argue, however, that even nomadic peoples have means of establishing provisional spatial boundaries, demarcations of inside and outside, us and them. Through human history up to very recent times, it is inconceivable that a sovereign "we" could be founded without spatial demarcation and, further,

enclosure. Today, we face a different configuration. Are the many virtual "we's" organized today by the Internet anticipatory of a new foundation for sovereign bodies?

10. Schmitt, *Nomos of the Earth*, pp. 82 and 94.

11. See Dictionary.com: An Ask.com service, at http://dictionary.reference. com/browse/beyond+the+pale (last accessed October 20, 2009).

12. Schmitt, *Nomos of the Earth*, pp. 78 and 98.

13. *Ibid.*, *Nomos of the Earth*, p. 70.

14. Paul Hirst, *Space and Power: Politics, War and Architecture* (Cambridge: Polity, 2005), pp. 184–85.

15. President George W. Bush, responding to a question by journalist Mark Trahant at the "Unity Conference" of minority journalists on August 10, 2004, available on-line at http://www.democracynow.org/2004/8/10/ bush_on_native_american_issues_tribal (last accessed October 20, 2009).

16. See, for example, Jens Bartelson, *A Genealogy of Sovereignty* (Cambridge: Cambridge University Press, 1995), pp. 16–17, and 24; and Jacques Derrida, *Rogues: Two Essays on Reason*, trans. Pachale-Anne Brault and Michael Naas (Stanford, CA: Stanford University Press, 2005), p. 15.

17. "Partial sovereignty" was described by the United States Department of State as the goal for Iraq in 2005. Derrida insists that sovereignty is always already partial and disunified. See *Rogues*.

18. The extreme of this appears in Rousseau, whose placement of the people's sovereignty and the state's power in two different books of *The Social Contract* has confused novice readers for centuries.

19. This tendency is evident in a range of thinkers, including Giorgio Agamben in *States of Exception*, trans. Kevin Attell (Chicago: University of Chicago Press, 2005), Michael Hardt and Antonio Negri in *Empire* (Cambridge, MA: Harvard University Press, 2000), Judith Butler in *Precarious Life: The Powers of Mourning and Violence* (London: Verso, 2004), and Mike Davis in "The Great Wall of Capital," in Michael Sorkin (ed.), *Against the Wall: Israel's Barrier to Peace* (New York: New Press, 2005). William Connolly works to finesse this problem by positing what he variously terms "ambiguity," "equivocation," and "oscillation" in sovereignty in general and an "uncertain circulation" in the sovereignty characteristic of democratic constitutional states. William Connolly, *Pluralism* (Durham, NC: Duke University Press, 2005), p. 140.

NOTES

According to Connolly, there is an "equivocation inside the idea of sovereignty between acting with final authority and acting with irresistible effect," an "oscillation between a juridical authority that decides the exception…and other cultural forces that insert themselves irresistibly into the outcome," the uncertain circulation of sovereignty "between authoritative sites of enunciation and irresistible forces of power," and, "in democratic constitutional states, sovereignty['s] circulat[ion] between the multitude, traditions infused into it, and constitutionally sanctioned authorities" (pp. 140–41). Each of these claims is aimed at deconstructing and debunking the conceptual bid of sovereignty to represent an independent and supreme power. They are ways of saying that sovereignty as it has been defined by others does not really exist, but is at best the conditioned site of a conditioned decision. This approach to sovereignty is part and parcel of Connolly's larger rejection of systems, logics, and absolutes in both language and politics.

20. Immanuel Kant, *Perpetual Peace*, trans. L. W. Beck (Indianapolis, IN: Bobbs-Merrill, 1957), p. 19.

21. Agamben has famously formulated this first type of sovereignty in terms of a permanent state of exception today. See Giorgio Agamben, *Homo Sacer: Sovereign Power and Bare Life*, trans. Daniel Heller-Roazen (Stanford, CA: Stanford University Press, 1998).

22. Locke, *Two Treatises of Government*, ch. 14, esp. paras. 166–67.

23. Connolly, *Pluralism*, ch. 5.

24. Eyal Weizman urges us to think otherwise. Given the political impossibility of conventional "one-state" and "two-state" solutions to the Israel-Palestine conflict at this point, he writes: "we would like to propose the idea of a simultaneous overlap: two states that are not lying side by side but overlap legally across the same territory. This obviously entails a new definition of national sovereignty, one in which a choice of more than one citizenship is available for the same area." Eyal Weizman, "The Wall and the Eye," an interview with Sina Najafi and Jeffrey Kastner, *Cabinet Magazine* 9 (Winter 2002), p. 31. Provocative as Weizman's suggestion is, I wonder if it is really a new formulation of sovereignty that makes sense here, or perhaps instead a new variety of federalism.

25. See Sheldon S. Wolin, "Fugitive Democracy," in Seyla Benhabib (ed.), *Democracy and Difference: Contesting the Boundaries of the Political* (Princeton,

145

NJ: Princeton University Press, 2002), and also developed in Sheldon S. Wolin, *Politics and Vision*, revised and expanded edition (Princeton, NJ: Princeton University Press, 2004).

26. Derrida, *Rogues*, p. 39.

27 . Schmitt calls sovereignty a "borderline concept," but means something else by this ascription: "a borderline concept is not a vague concept, but one pertaining to the outermost sphere. This definition of sovereignty [the sovereign is he who decides on the exception] must therefore be associated with a borderline case and not with routine." Carl Schmitt, *Political Theology: Four Chapters on the Concept of Sovereignty*, trans. George Schwab (Cambridge, MA: The MIT Press, 1985), p. 5.

28. *Webster's* gives "supreme power especially over a political unit" as the first modern definition of sovereignty and "freedom from external control" as the second. *Webster's Collegiate Dictionary*, 15th ed., s.v. "sovereignty."

29. Stephen Krasner attempts to discredit the historical association of sovereignty with supreme power and reduces its meaning to "the idea that states are autonomous and independent from each other." See Stephen D. Krasner, "Sovereignty," *Foreign Policy* (January/February 2001), available on-line at www.globalpolicy.org/component/content/article/172/30357.html (last accessed October 20, 2009).

30. Schmitt writes, "What characterizes an exception is principally unlimited authority, which means the suspension of the entire existing order. In such a situation it is clear that the state remains, whereas law recedes. Because the exception is different from anarchy and chaos, order in the juristic sense still prevails even if it is not of the ordinary kind. The existence of the state is undoubted proof of its superiority over the validity of the legal norm. The decision frees itself from all normative ties and becomes in the true sense absolute. The state suspends the law in the exception on the basis of its right of self-preservation.... The two elements of the concept *legal order* are then dissolved into independent notions and thereby testify to their conceptual independence." Schmitt, *Political Theology*, p. 12.

31. Hegel writes: "The term 'popular sovereignty' may be used to indicate that a people is self-sufficient for all *external* purposes and constitutes a state of its own.... We may also say that *internal sovereignty* lies with the *people* but only if we are speaking of the whole [state] in general, in keeping with the

[argument] that sovereignty belongs to the *state*. But the usual sense in which the term 'popular sovereignty' has begun to be used in recent times is to denote *the opposite of that sovereignty which exists in the monarch*. In this oppositional sense, popular sovereignty is one of those confused thoughts which are based on a garbled notion of the people. *Without* its monarch and that *articulation* of the whole which is necessarily and immediately associated with monarchy, *the people is a formless mass*." G. W. F. Hegel, *Elements of the Philosophy of Right*, ed. Allen Wood, trans. H. B. Nisbet (Cambridge: Cambridge University Press, 1991), para. 279, pp. 318–19.

32. See Bartelson, *Genealogy of Sovereignty*, pp. 28 and 48.

33. See Agamben, *Homo Sacer*; Hardt and Negri, *Empire*; and Connolly, *Pluralism*.

34. Jean Bodin, *On Sovereignty: Four Chapters from the Six Books of the Commonwealth*, ed. and trans. Julian H. Franklin (Cambridge: Cambridge University Press, 1992), pp. 2, 3, 12–13, 71.

35. This claim differs substantially from the Hardt and Negri thesis that sovereignty entails the conjoining of the political and the economic, the service of the former to the latter (or the supply of economic content to political form), and that sovereignty is born out of secularism.

36. The friend-enemy distinction is the ultimate and singular distinction that defines the political, expressing not merely its essence, but what marks its difference from other fields. See Carl Schmitt, *The Concept of the Political*, trans. George Schwab (Chicago: University of Chicago Press, 1996), p. 26.

37. Schmitt, *Political Theology*, p. 5.

38. Schmitt acknowledges political enmity may acquire a moral, juridical, or economic character, but that this acquisition is secondary if the enmity is political. See *Concept of the Political*, p. 38.

39. Schmitt is not alone here. Most anxieties about the "death of the political" center on the eroded autonomy, purity, or sovereignty of the political. For Max Weber, this threat emanated from bureaucracy and rationalization, for Hannah Arendt, from the rise of the social and *animal laborans*, for Machiavelli, from both religion and corruption by private interests.

40. Here is John Stuart Mill in the opening of book 4 of *On Liberty*: "What, then, is the rightful limit to the sovereignty of the individual over himself? Where does the authority of society begin? How much of human life should

be assigned to individuality, and how much to society?" (New York: Hackett, 1978), p. 73. Or consider Thomas Hobbes's argument in *Leviathan* that the individual is free where "the laws are silent" or John Locke's efforts to delineate the respective jurisdictions of religious and state authority in the *Letter on Toleration*. See Thomas Hobbes, *Leviathan*, ed. C. B. MacPherson (London: Penguin, 1981) and John Locke, *Political Essays*, ed. Mark Goldie (Cambridge: Cambridge University Press, 1997).

41. This would seem to erode one of the crucial distinctions that Foucault uses to hold sovereignty apart from biopower and suggests instead that sovereignty sometimes operates in the modality of biopower.

42. In his unique origin story for the social contract in *What is the Third Estate?* Abbé Sieyès argues that sovereignty emerges to manage the political life of *homo oeconomicus* and yet detaches from these economic origins as it comes into its own. This detachment is also crucial to the theological form that sovereignty takes. My gratitude goes to graduate student Asaf Kedar for bringing this to my attention in a first-rate seminar paper written in the fall of 2005.

43. Hardt and Negri, *Empire*, pp. 85–86. Hardt and Negri assert this claim without developing it. It appears to be mostly a Marxist reflex on their part.

44. Schmitt, *Political Theology*, p. 36.

45. Hobbes, *Leviathan*, "Introduction," p. 81.

46. See Norman Jacobson, "Behold Leviathan!" in *Pride and Solace: The Functions and Limits of Political Theory* (Berkeley: University of California Press, 1977), pp. 53–54.

47. Hobbes, *Leviathan*, "Introduction," p. 81.

48. *Ibid.*, ch. 13, p. 185.

49. Consider these lines from *What is the Third Estate?* in Emmanuel Joseph Sieyes, *Political Writings* (Indianapolis, IN: Hackett, 2003), ch. 1:

"The nation exists prior to everything; it is the origin of everything. Its will is always legal. It is the law itself."

"A nation is all that it can be simply by virtue of being what it is."

"However a nation may will, it is enough for it to will. Every form is good, and its will is always the supreme law."

"A nation is independent of all forms and, however it may will, it is enough for its will to be made known for all positive law to fall silent in its presence, because it is the source and supreme master of all positive law."

148

50. Bodin, *On Sovereignty*, p. 45.

51. In the following account of American actions abroad, note Bush's striking conflations of God and state, authorship and interpellation, sovereign utterances and holy truth: "I believe the United States is *the* beacon for freedom in the world. And I believe we have a responsibility to promote freedom. [But] freedom is not America's gift to the world. Freedom is God's gift to everybody in the world. I believe that. As a matter of fact, I was the person that wrote the line, or said it. I didn't write it, I just said it in a speech. And it became part of the jargon. And I believe that. And I believe we have a duty to free people." George W. Bush, speaking to Bob Woodward, in Bob Woodward, *Plan of Attack* (New York: Simon and Schuster, 2004), pp. 88–89.

52. Barack Obama, press conference, May 18, 2009, available on-line at http://www.whitehouse.gov/the_press_office/Remarks-by-President-Obama-and-Israeli-Prime-Minister-Netanyahu-in-press-availability (last accessed October 22, 2009).

53. Hannah Arendt, *Origins of Totalitarianism* (New York: Harcourt, 1951); Agamben, *Homo Sacer.*

54. For the neoliberals, "democracy" is identified with the embrace of this sovereign. Their designation of Iraq as a democracy, amid its political and economic rebuilding by Paul Bremer and foreign investment, is only one of the more blatant examples. See Wendy Brown, "Neoliberalism and the End of Liberal Democracy," in *Edgework: Critical Essays on Knowledge and Politics* (Princeton, NJ: Princeton University Press, 2005).

55. In a work in progress on Marx's critique of religion, I disagree with this account of capital and of a reading of Marx that subscribes to it. For a preview of this work, see Wendy Brown, "The Sacred, the Secular and the Profane: Charles Taylor and Karl Marx," in Jonathan van Antwerpen, et al. (eds.), *Varieties of Secularism in a Secular Age* (Cambridge, MA: Harvard University Press, 2010).

56. Saskia Sassen, *Losing Control?: Sovereignty in an Age of Globalization* (New York: Columbia University Press, 1996), p. xii.

57. *Ibid.*, p. xiv.

58. Derrida, *Rogues*, p. 102.

59. Many political scientists have made similar arguments. See, for example, Chris Ansell and Steve Weber, "Organizing International Politics:

Sovereignty and Open Systems," *International Political Science Reviews* 10, no. 1 (1999): pp. 73–93.

60. Hannah Arendt, *The Origins of Totalitarianism*, pp. 295–96.

61. As Peter Andreas notes, there is no small irony in the First World hunkering down today against the disruptive economic, political, and cultural effects of globalization. A mere quarter century ago, Third World nations complained most about neoliberalism's often deformative effects on national economic development, social and political structures, political autonomy, and citizen well-being. Today, Andreas writes, it is "the advanced industrialized states that are building up their protective walls against two of the developing world's leading exports: drugs and migrant labor." Peter Andreas, *Border Games: Policing the U.S.-Mexico Divide*, 2nd ed. (Ithaca, NY: Cornell University Press, 2009), p. 141.

62. Sassen, *Losing Control?*, p. xii.

63. Secularism and secularization are heavily contested concepts, even among contemporary scholars. For a sample of this contestation, see William Connolly, *Why I am Not a Secularist* (Minneapolis: University of Minnesota Press, 1990); Talal Asad, *Formations of the Secular: Christianity, Islam, Modernity* (Stanford, CA: Stanford University Press, 2003); and Charles Taylor, *A Secular Age* (Cambridge, MA: Harvard University Press, 2007).

64. "The exception in jurisprudence is analogous to the miracle in theology." Schmitt, *Political Theology*, p. 36. Hobbes, *Leviathan*, pp. 263–64; Bodin, *On Sovereignty*, p. 46.

65. Derrida, *Rogues*, p. 81.

CHAPTER THREE: STATES AND SUBJECTS

1. Edward Said, *Orientalism* (New York: Vintage, 1979), p. 54.

2. Paul Hirst, *Space and Power: Politics, War and Architecture* (Cambridge: Polity, 2005), pp. 158 and 190.

3. Nelson Goodman, "How Buildings Mean," in Nelson Goodman and Catherine Z. Elgin (eds.), *Reconceptions in Philosophy and Other Arts and Sciences* (Indianapolis, IN: Hackett, 1988), pp. 32 and 34.

4. Said, *Orientalism*, p. 55.

5. Quoted in Marita Sturken, "The Wall, the Screen, and the Image," *Representations* 35 (Summer 1991): pp. 122 and 124.

6. Paul Virilio, *Bunker Archeology*, trans. George Collins (Princeton, NJ: Princeton Architectural Press, 2008), p. 46. See also Keith Mallory and Arvid Ottar, *Walls of War: A History of Military Architecture in North West Europe 1900–1945* (London: Astragal Books, 1973).

7. Trevor Boddy, "Architecture Emblematic: Hardened Sites and Softened Symbols," in Michael Sorkin (ed.), *Indefensible Space: The Architecture of the National Insecurity State* (New York: Routledge, 2008), pp. 281–82.

8. *Ibid.*, p. 281.

9. However sophisticated and sleek, this architecture still lacks efficacy vis-à-vis the dangers that 9/11 brought to the fore. It does not deal with pedestrian suicide bombers, biological weapons, airplane hijackers, and so on. To date, car bombs have been rare in the United States and have been used only by domestic terrorists, notably the Weathermen and Timothy McVeigh (the "Oklahoma City bomber").

10. Thomas Hobbes, *Leviathan*, ed. C.B. MacPherson (London: Penguin, 1981), ch. 13, p. 186. Thus does the promise of protection through state sovereignty both originally and continuously justify the surrender of natural liberty and independence in making the social contract. This surrender produces a new form of individual sovereignty that we might call "civil sovereignty." The exchange might be considered analogous to the moral and civil freedom Rousseau argues we acquire for giving up our natural liberty and is similarly dependent upon the powers of protection offered by political sovereignty.

11. The "peace lines"—walls ranging in length from a few hundred meters to several kilometers, made of iron, brick, and steel and adorned with remarkable political murals—separate Protestant and Catholic neighborhoods in Belfast, Derry, and other parts of Northern Ireland. Construction on them began in the early 1970s and has continued through the present.

12. Peter Andreas, "Redrawing the Line: Borders and Security in the Twenty-first Century," *International Security* 28, no. 2 (Fall 2003): p. 78; and *Border Games: Policing the U.S.-Mexico Divide* (Ithaca, NY: Cornell University Press, 2000).

13. Valéry Giscard d'Estaing, *Le Figaro Magazine*, September 21, 1991, cited in Jane Freedman, *Immigration and Insecurity in France* (Aldershot, UK: Ashgate, 2004), p. 17.

14. Reversing the trends of the past two centuries, most Western

democracies have backed away from universal citizenship in recent decades and in particular from welcoming the enfranchisement of new arrivals. Not only France and Germany, but the United States, Australia, and the Netherlands, all lands with a history of welcoming and incorporating immigrants and refugees, have recently "widened the gulf in rights and entitlements between nationals and non-nationals" and have promulgated more, rather than less exclusive models of citizenship. Freedman, *Immigration and Insecurity in France*, p. 14. Cultural and political thresholds for citizenship have been raised, including not only language proficiency but, as in the case of the Netherlands, attitudes toward homosexuality, nudity, and gender equality.

15. Carl Schmitt, *The Concept of the Political*, trans. George Schwab (Chicago: University of Chicago Press, 1996), p. 26; Carl Schmitt, *Political Theology: Four Chapters on the Concept of Sovereignty*, trans. George Schwab (Chicago: University of Chicago Press, 2005), p. 5.

16. Andreas, *Border Games*, 7.

17. Yuli Tamir, "Protection in the Territories," *Ha'aretz*, March 18, 2003, cited in Derek Gregory, *The Colonial Present: Afghanistan, Palestine, Iraq* (Oxford: Blackwell, 2004), p. 131.

18. Georgio Agamben, *Homo Sacer: Sovereign Power and Bare Life*, trans. Daniel Heller-Roazen (Stanford, CA: Stanford University Press, 1998); and *State of Exception*, trans. Kevin Attell (Chicago: University of Chicago Press, 2005).

19. Lars Buur, discussing vigilantism in the South African context, refers to this blurring as "the outsourcing of sovereignty" and formulates its effect, wrongly in my view, as extending, rather than undermining sovereignty. Lars Buur, "The Sovereign Outsourced: Local Justice and Violence in Port Elizabeth" in Thomas Blom Hansen and Finn Stepputat (eds.), *Sovereign Bodies: Citizens, Migrants, and States in the Postcolonial World* (Princeton, NJ: Princeton University Press, 2005).

20. "Minuteman Border Fence," available on-line at http://www.minutemanhq.com/bf/pl10.php (last accessed October 24, 2009).

21. *Ibid.*

22. BBC News, "Web Users to 'Patrol' US Border," June 2, 2006, available on-line at http://news.bbc.co.uk/2/hi/americas/5040372.stm (last accessed October 24, 2009).

23. This paradox is also sometimes carried in walls themselves: High,

opaque walls provide cover for and make more difficult direct surveillance of criminal activity along the "wrong" side of the border. Yet translucent or virtual fences are not only less politically imposing and hence less useful for producing a sovereign imago, they render border patrols and other guards more vulnerable to assaults, whether by armed smugglers or armed insurgents.

24. See http://www.usborderpatrol.com (last accessed October 24, 2009).

25. *Ibid.*, now removed from the site.

26. Quoted in Leo W. Banks, "Let's Climb the Wall," *Tucson Weekly*, June 19, 2008, available on-line at http://www.tucsonweekly.com/tucson/Currents/Content?oid=oid%3A112135 (last accessed October 24, 2009).

27. Mike Davis, "The Great Wall of Capital," in Michael Sorkin (ed.), *Against the Wall: Israel's Barrier to Peace* (New York: New Press, 2005), p. 90.

28. Andreas, *Border Games*, pp. 143 and 144.

29. Davis, "The Great Wall of Capital," p. 91.

30. Andreas, *Border Games*, p. 148.

31. Quoted in Banks, "Let's Climb the Wall."

32. Jagdish N. Bhagwati, "U.S. Immigration Policy: What Next?" in Susan Pozo (ed.), *Essays on Legal and Illegal Immigration* (Kalamazoo, MI: W. E. Upjohn Institute for Employment Research, 1986), p. 124, cited in Andreas, *Border Games*, p. 148.

33. Joseph Nevins, *Operation Gatekeeper: The Rise of the "Illegal Alien" and the Making of the U.S.-Mexico Boundary* (New York: Routledge, 2002), p. 176.

34. Schmitt, *Political Theology*, p. 10.

35. *Ibid.*, p. 12.

36. U.S. Department of Homeland Security press release, "Action Plan for Creating a Secure and Smart Border," December 12, 2001, available on-line at http://www.dhs.gov/xnews/releases/press_release_0037.shtm (last accessed October 24, 2009).

37. Mathew Coleman, "U.S. Statecraft and the U.S.-Mexico Border as Security/Economy Nexus," *Political Geography* 24, no. 2 (2005): p. 189.

38. Naomi Klein, *Shock Doctrine: The Rise of Disaster Capitalism* (New York: Picador, 2007), "Introduction."

39. Hannah Arendt, "The Perplexities of the Rights of Man," in *Origins of Totalitarianism* (New York: Harcourt, 1966), pp. 290–302. While powerful in many ways, aside from empirical inaccuracies, Arendt's analysis is limited by

her treatment of this production as an exclusively political phenomenon. She occludes the way that, even in the period about which she was writing, "statelessness" was produced by economic dislocation, and not only by nationalistic "ethnic cleansing" projects related to fusing the state to the nation.

40. Michel Foucault, *The Birth of Biopolitics: Lectures at the College de France, 1978–79*, ed. Arnold Davidson (Basingstoke, UK: Palgrave Macmillan, 2008). See also Thomas Lemke, "'The Birth of Bio-Politics': Michel Foucault's Lecture at the College de France on Neoliberal Governmentality," *Economy and Society* 30, no. 2 (May 2001).

41. On specks of human capital, see Michel Feher, "Self-Appreciation, or the Aspirations of Human Capital," *Public Culture* 21, no. 1 (2009).

42. For a fuller discussion of neoliberal rationality and its corrosive effect on the rule of law, see my "Neoliberalism and the End of Liberal Democracy" in *Edgework* (Princeton, NJ: Princeton University Press, 2007). See also Michel Feher, "Self-Appreciation," and Pierre Dardot and Christian Laval, *La nouvelle raison du monde: Essai sur la societé neoliberale* (Paris: La Decouverte, 2009).

43. Lemke, "'The Birth of Bio-Politics,'" p. 199.

44. Davis, "Great Wall of Capital," pp. 91, 98–99.

45. Davis, "Great Wall of Capital," p. 91.

46. Jack Ladd, quoted in Banks, "Let's Climb the Wall."

47. Anita Vittulo, "The Long Economic Shadow of the Wall," in Sorkin (ed.), *Against the Wall*, p. 101. Like immigration policy in the United States, policy concerning West Bank Palestinians coming into Israel to work is heavily debated. The Gaza Disengagement Plan called for completely eliminating the flow of Palestinian workers entering Israel. That said, it seems no more likely that Israel can function without Palestinian labor than New York's Upper West Side can function without West Indians, California agriculture and construction can function without Mexicans, or Europe can function without its "inassimilable Arabs." Striking in this respect is the use of Palestinian workers to build the Wall and Israeli settlers' employment of Palestinian domestic labor.

48. *Ibid.*

49. Lindsey Bremner, "Border/Skin," in Sorkin (ed.), *Against the Wall*, p. 131.

50. Ruchama Marton and Dalit Baum, "Transparent Wall, Opaque Gates," in Sorkin (ed.), *Against the Wall*, p. 216.

51. See, for example, the story of Indian rice farmers separated from their farmland by the wall sealing off Kashmir from Pakistan. Rama Lakshmi, "India's Border Fence Extended to Kashmir," *Washington Post*, July 30, 2003.

52. The Fourth Geneva Convention prohibits the building of permanent settlements on occupied land, but permits temporary installations built in the name of security. The Peres government seized on this distinction both to promote and to defend the settlements in the late 1970s. And the Israeli High Court of Justice backed Peres, arguing that "with respect to pure military considerations, there is no doubt that the presence of settlements, even if 'civilian,' of the occupying power in the occupying territory substantially contributes to the security in that area and facilitates the execution of the duties of the military." As Eyal Weizman concludes, "here the court is clearly establishing the fact that civilians and residential settlements could have a security function that is normally attributed to the police and the army." Sina Najafi and Jeffrey Kastner, "The Wall and the Eye: An Interview with Eyal Weizman," *Cabinet Magazine* 9 (Winter 2002), p. 24.

53. This is a common billboard poster in the Southwest of the United States, and pictures of the billboard appear on a number of profence Web sites, including those of the Minutemen and Weneedafence.com.

54. "Ask Our Leaders to Secure Our Borders Immediately," We Need a Fence Blog, Monday, October 3, 2005, available on-line at http://weneedafence. blogspot.com (last accessed October 24, 2009).

55. See http://weneedafence.blogspot.com/2006/05/open-border-poem-by-scott-rohter.html (last accessed October 24, 2009).

56. The line they draw between the safe interior and dangerous exterior is blurred by the security architecture and apparatuses extended deep inside the nation and by the mobilization of citizens everywhere for war against the alien, both of which give the lie to the safe interior Rohter invokes.

57. Davis, "The Great Wall of Capital," p. 91.

58. For Hobbes, sovereignty is a literal imitation of God's power. More than governing, it is the only human power that subjects us by overawing. *Leviathan*, p. 185. From his appreciation that belief, like reason, is not uniform in its reach or effects, Hobbes moved to supplement awe based on belief when building the political sovereign: The supplement is fear.

59. Consider the lines ending the first stanza of Rohter's poem, "I pray,

keep safe this land of mine," and commencing the second, "Consider this, that it's your job."

CHAPTER FOUR: DESIRING WALLS

1. Cited in Randal C. Archibold, "Along the Border, Smugglers Build an Underground World," *New York Times*, December 7, 2007, A-18.

2. See especially Eyal Weizman, *Hollow Land: Israel's Architecture of Occupation* (London: Verso, 2007); and Neve Gordon, *Israel's Occupation* (Berkeley: University of California Press, 2009).

3. Jason Ackleson, "Constructing Security on the U.S.-Mexico Border," *Political Geography* 24, no. 2 (2005): pp. 165–84.

4. "Border Fence Firm Snared for Hiring Illegal Workers," *All Things Considered*, National Public Radio, Scott Horsley, December 14, 2006. The five-million-dollar fine Golden State ultimately paid was a pittance compared with the market share and profit it derived from these practices over a decade.

5. Weizman, *Hollow Land*, p. 169.

6. Peter Andreas, *Border Games: Policing the US-Mexico Divide* (Ithaca, NY: Cornell University Press, 2000), p. 146.

7. For an account of recent tunneling production at the U.S.-Mexico border, see Archibold, "Along the Border, Smugglers Build an Underground World."

8. Teddy Cruz, "Border Tours" in Michael Sorkin (ed.), *Indefensible Space: The Architecture of the National Insecurity State* (New York: Routledge, 2008), and Archibold, "Along the Border, Smugglers Build an Underground World."

9. "First US-Mexico Border Fence Sees Fewer Migrants, More Violence" *Dallas News*, September 13, 2008.

10. *Ibid.*

11. Jesse McKinley and Malia Wollan, "New Border Fear: Violence by a Rogue Militia," *New York Times*, June 27, 2009, A1, 9.

12. Blas Nunez-Neto and Yule Kim, *Border Security: Barriers along the U.S. International Border* (Washington, D.C.: Congressional Research Service, 2008) and "Administration Moves to Bypass Laws to Complete Mexico Border Fence this Year," *Guardian*, April 1, 2008.

13. Benedict Anderson, *Imagined Communities: Reflections on the Origin and Spread of Nationalism* (London: Verso, 1991), pp. 6–7.

14. There are other important questions provoked by the phenomenon of walling today in the face of its inefficacy, though they are slightly tangential to the problematic of sovereignty. How does the desire for walls comport with discourses about extending and even instantiating democracy across the globe? How does it square with the premises of openness and universality entailed by this project? Alternatively, what kind of containment might the desire for walls indicate that democracy requires? Is there a new formulation of democracy here ... or revival of an ancient one?

15. Mary Douglas, *Purity and Danger: An Analysis of Concepts of Pollution and Taboo* (London: Routledge and Kegan Paul, 1966).

16. Quoted in John Dougherty, "Census: 100,000 Mideast Illegals in U.S. Analysts Say Failure of Immigration Control Contributed to 9-11 Attacks," WorldNetDaily, http://www.wnd.com/news/article.asp?ARTICLE_ID=26194 (last accessed October 25, 2009).

17. Samuel Huntington, *The Clash of Civilizations and the Remaking of World Order* (New York: Simon and Schuster, 1997), pp. 304–305.

18. *Ibid.*, p. 306.

19. Robert J. Sampson, "Rethinking Crime and Immigration," *Contexts* 7 (Winter 2008), and "Open Doors Don't Invite Criminals: Is Increased Immigration Behind the Drop in Crime?" *New York Times* Op-Ed, March 11, 2006, p. A27.

20. Hannah Arendt, *The Human Condition* (Chicago: University of Chicago Press, 1958).

21. Nietzsche, "Uses and Disadvantages of History for Life" in *Untimely Meditations*, trans. R. J. Hollingdale (Cambridge: Cambridge University Press, 1983), p. 63.

22. In "Building Dwelling Thinking," (1952) Heidegger writes: "What the word for space, *Raum*, *Rum*, designates is said by its ancient meaning. *Raum* means a place cleared or freed for settlement and lodging. A space is something that has been made room for, something that is cleared and free, namely within a boundary, Greek *peras*. A boundary is not that which something stops but, as the Greeks recognized, the boundary is that from which something *begins its presencing*. That is why the concept is that of *horismos*, that is, the horizon, the boundary. Space is in essence that for which room has been made, that which is let into its bounds." Martin Heidegger, "Building Dwelling Thinking," in

Poetry, Language, Thought, trans. Albert Hofstadter (New York: Harper and Row, 1971), p. 154.

23. On the state as container, see Anthony Giddens, *The Nation-State and Violence* (Cambridge: Polity, 1985), and Peter J. Taylor, "The State as Container: Territoriality in the Modern World-System," *Progress in Human Geography* 18, no. 2 (1994): pp. 151–62.

24. Achille Mbembe, "Sovereignty as a Form of Expenditure," in Thomas Blom Hansen and Finn Stepputat (eds.), *Sovereign Bodies: Citizens, Migrants, and States in the Postcolonial World* (Princeton, NJ: Princeton University Press, 2005), pp. 161–63.

25. Saskia Sassen, *Losing Control?: Sovereignty in an Age of Globalization* (New York: Columbia University Press, 1996).

26. Paul Hirst, *Space and Power* (Cambridge: Polity, 2005), ch. 10.

27. "The cheap prices of commodities are the heavy artillery with which [the bourgeoisie] batters down all Chinese walls, with which it forces the barbarians' intensely obstinate hatred of foreigners to capitulate." Karl Marx, "Manifesto of the Communist Party," *The Marx-Engels Reader*, 2nd ed., ed. Robert C. Tucker (New York: Norton, 1978), p. 477.

28. Israeli Ministry of Foreign Affairs, "Saving Lives—Israel's Anti-Terrorist Fence: Answers to Questions," January 1, 2004, available on-line at http://www.mfa.gov.il/mfa/mfaarchive/2000_2009/2003/11/saving%20lives-%20israel-s%20anti-terrorist%20fence%20-%20answ (last accessed October 25, 2009).

29. See http://www.weneedafence.com; http://www.americanpatrol.com; and http://www.borderfenceproject.com (all last accessed October 25, 2009).

30. Ruchama Marton and Dalit Baum, "Transparent Wall, Opaque Gates," in Michael Sorkin (ed.), *Against the Wall: Israel's Barrier to Peace* (New York: New Press, 2005), p. 215.

31. In these early papers, Freud is embarrassingly quantitative about this process, referring to the "sum" or "quantity" of "excitation" in the original desire having to be redirected.

32. Sigmund Freud, "The Neuro-Psychoses of Defence" in the *Standard Edition of the Complete Psychological Works of Sigmund Freud*, trans. and ed. James Strachey, 24 vols. (London: Hogarth Press, 1953–64), vol. 3, p. 47.

33. *Ibid.*, pp. 49, 50, 52–53.

34. Anna Freud, *The Ego and the Mechanisms of Defense*, trans. Cecil Baines (New York: International Universities Press, 1946), pp. 45–46.

35. *Ibid.*, p. 47.

36. *Ibid.*, pp. 54–55. She also adds that certain defense mechanisms can be employed early in childhood (regression, reversal, turning against oneself) while others, like sublimation, require more maturity because they entail acceptance of certain values (p. 56).

37. *Ibid.*, p. 64.

38. *Ibid.*, p. 65.

39. *Ibid.*, pp. 73, 74.

40. *Ibid.*, pp. 7–8.

41. Carl Schmitt, *Nomos of the Earth in the International Law of the Jus Publicum Europaeum*, trans. G. L. Ulmen (New York: Telos Press, 2006), p. 45.

42. Anna Freud, *The Ego and the Mechanisms of Defense*, p. 35.

43. Anna Freud says the ego is defended against at least three things: the id, the analyst, the affects associated with instinct (*ibid.*, pp. 32–33). The ego is not all that is modified by the defenses. The instincts against which the defenses are built also are transformed by them. Consequently, "only the analysis of the ego's unconscious defensive operations can enable us to reconstruct transformations which the instincts have undergone" (p. 27). Active identities on both sides of the fence are produced by the defenses, which is why these identities become the crucial texts through which the instincts can be read. Even here, the defenses themselves are not always easy to see, and "reaction-formation can best be studied when such formations are in the process of disintegration" (p. 10). So there is a reading of the id available only through the transformations that the defenses have produced in the defenses themselves and through a consideration of the particular methods of defense that are deployed (p. 27), but it is also the case that certain readings of the defenses are available only when they are falling apart, even when psychosis is on the horizon (p. 10). The recognition that defense makes analysis itself impossible led Wilhelm Reich in *Character Analysis*, trans. Vincent R. Carfagno (New York: Macmillan, 1980), to insist that psychoanalysis has to work directly on the defense mechanism itself, and not simply analyze its content or source.

44. Anna Freud, *The Ego and the Mechanisms of Defense*, p. 61.

45. *Ibid.*, pp. 73, 34.

46. Ehud Barak, quoted in Akiva Eldar, "A Visit to the Jungle," *Ha'aretz*, January 28, 2009, available on-line at http://www.haaretz.com/hasen/ spages/890295.html (last accessed October 27, 2009).

47. Azmi Bishara, *Checkpoints: Fragments of a Story* (Tel Aviv: Babel Press, 2006) (in Hebrew), p. 10, cited in Weizman, *Hollow Land*, p. 147.

48. Anna Freud distinguishes sharply between the functions and purview of denial and repression, arguing that the former is for external danger, the latter for internal conflict. See *The Ego and the Mechanisms of Defense*, pp. 45–47 and 190–91.

49. Guy Debord, *Society of the Spectacle*, trans. Donald Nicholson-Smith (New York: Zone Books, 1995), thesis 5.

50. Sigmund Freud, *The Future of an Illusion*, trans. W. D. Robson-Scott (Garden City, NY: Doubleday, 1964), pp. 23–26.

51. *Ibid.*, pp. 48–49.

52. This insight reveals the illusory power of science as it attempts to reveal religion as an illusion, though this is not a matter Freud pursues.

53. Freud, *The Future of an Illusion*, pp. 49, 55.

Index

United States, 102; militarization of life
in, 42; as nation settled by immigrants,
103; settlers in occupied Palestinian
territories, 64, 84–85, 155 n.52; Sinai
Desert border with Egypt, 20, 28;
singular history of, 33–35; "special
relationship" with United States, 62–63;
theological dimension of sovereignty
and, 62–64.
Israeli security fence ("the Wall"), 28–35,
80, 140 n.14; activists and protestors
against, 31, 122, 137 n.1; "depth barriers"
and, 30, 32; discourses associated with,
76; images of, 12–13; inefficacy of, 110;
Palestinian economy and, 100–101;
psychoanalytic defense theory and, 130;
public relations for, 121–22; security
dilemmas of, 100; sovereignty and, 34;
state of exception and, 85; suspension
of law and, 87; territorial expansion
and, 28, 29, 101; ugliness projected onto
other, 122–23; U.S.–Mexico border wall
and, 8, 28, 32, 38–39, 137 n.1.
Ivins, Bruce, 117.

"JERSEY BARRIERS," 76, 77, 78.
Jerusalem, city of, 19, 30, 86, 143 n.3.
Jews, 62, 63, 74, 76, 99.

KANT, IMMANUEL, 44, 49, 138 n.5.
Kashmir, 8, 30, 85.
Katrina, Hurricane, 95.
Klein, Naomi, 95.
Korea, Cold War boundary in, 47.
Korea, North, 19.
Krasner, Stephen, 146 n.29.
Kuwait, 20.
Kyrgyzstan, 8, 28.

LABOR, 68, 98, 150 n.61; cheap labor,
25, 99, 117, 129; globally dispersed
sources of, 83; guest-worker policies, 99;
transnational flows of, 62, 95; U.S.–
Mexico border wall and, 30, 36, 37, 111.
Law and legal discourses, 23, 54;
international law, 23; property and,
44; rule of law, 22, 38, 48, 50, 53, 70;
suspension of law, 31, 38, 40, 48, 87.
Legitimation, 27, 31, 33, 34–35, 122.

Lemke, Thomas, 97.
Liberalism, 48, 53, 120–21, 131.
Limbang, 19.
Locke, John, 44, 48, 50, 56, 79, 148 n.40.

MACHIAVELLI, NICCOLÒ, 7, 44, 147 n.39.
Maginot Line, 40, 73.
Malaysia, border with Thailand, 19.
Markets, global, 8, 20.
Marx, Karl, 51, 131, 149 n.55.
Marxism, 21, 65.
Masculinity/masculinism, 88, 108, 119–20.
Mbembe, Achille, 118–19.
McCain, John, 107.
McVeigh, Timothy, 151 n.9.
Melilla enclave (Morocco), 9, 28, 32.
Mexico, 10, 11, 19, 20, 30, 32, 35–42,
86, 137 nn.1, 4, 138 n.8, 140 n.17,
142 n.28.
Middle Ages, 120.
Middle East, 28, 62–63.
Militarism, phallic, 119.
Mill, John Stuart, 56, 147–48 n.40.
Minutemen vigilantes, 85, 87–88, 108,
113, 126.
Miranda rights, 89.
Modernity, 49, 56, 65.
Morocco: Spanish enclaves in, 9, 19, 28,
30, 32, 85; Western Sahara berm, 19,
28, 85, 90.
Multiculturalism, 116, 117.
Muslims, 63, 69, 116.

NAFTA (NORTH AMERICAN FREE TRADE
AGREEMENT), 120.
Napolitano, Janet, 107.
National interests, 8.
Nationalism, 8, 23, 38, 69, 108, 118.
Nation-states, 20, 21, 24; economic
regulation and, 57; emasculation of, 119,
125, 131; "failed" states, 83; flows and
barriers inside, 24; post-Westphalian
order and, 21; sovereignty separated
from, 66; state–subject relation,
108–109; threats to identity and powers
of, 27; walls as death of sovereignty,
43–44. See also Sovereignty.
Native Americans, 30, 36, 113.
Nazism, 40, 75.

Zone Books series design by Bruce Mau
Typesetting by Meighan Gale
Printed and bound by Thomson-Shore